BEYOND
FEMINISM

BEYOND FEMINISM

The Woman of Faith in Action

marilyn brown oden

NASHVILLE ABINGDON PRESS NEW YORK

BEYOND FEMINISM

Copyright © 1971 by Abingdon Press

ISBN 0-687-030323

Library of Congress Catalog Card Number: 70-134249

SET UP, PRINTED, AND BOUND BY THE
PARTHENON PRESS, AT NASHVILLE,
TENNESSEE, UNITED STATES OF AMERICA

To Mother

ACKNOWLEDGMENTS

I am indebted to many women for sharing their experiences and knowledge of what it means to try to be responsible in today's world. I would especially like to express my appreciation of:

Dr. Mary Abbott, excellent pediatrician and committed Christian, who is a model for all the little girls who go home from her office and play doctor instead of nurse.

Nancy (Mrs. James Dan) Batchelor, an attorney, who at this time primarily focuses on her preschool children and thereby affirms the importance of the various stages in a woman's life.

Panthea (Mrs. John) Freeman, one of the outstanding laywomen in the Oklahoma Conference of the United Methodist Church, who gives her life away through meaningful and significant volunteer roles.

Dr. Marilyn (Mrs. Philip) Ogilvie, historian of science, who touches life fully—from the seriousness and discipline required in her field to the spontaneity of a frolic with her children in the park.

Dr. Dorothy Truex, past Dean of Women at the University of Oklahoma, who shared with me her insight as a woman who is a professional in the world of academe.

The Mississippi Conference Methodist ministers' wives, for whom the basis of this material was written, and with whom I experienced a common struggle to live the faith in our day.

I want also to express my gratitude for those persons closest to me:

Bill, with whom it is my joy to share life and love and meaning and commitment.

Danna Lee, Dirk, Valerie Lyn, and Bryant, our children, whose fresh views of life penetrate my blindness to the simple majesty that exists within our complex society.

The members of the St. Stephen's United Methodist Church, an open, flexible, cooperative congregation, from whom I have received far more than I have given.

CONTENTS

FOREWORD

Human beings have a habit of creating false alternatives when faced with difficult decisions. These add to the polarizations which mark our era. In no question is this more apparent than in current discussions about the role of women in today's world. One alternative, passionately espoused by many men and women, is the traditional role of wife, mother, homemaker, helpmeet to man. It is described incisively by Mrs. Oden, and labeled the "mistress-madonna" role. The other extreme is the "imitator of the male" role, equally strongly advocated and defended by the militant feminists working for the liberation of women.

Mrs. Oden's theme considers the possibility of another alternative: modern woman as "innovator." She makes a clear and convincing case that a woman today need not accept either of the extreme alternatives, but has both the freedom and the responsibility to carve out a new and creative life-style which builds on all the strengths of femininity and all the amazing possibilities open to a responsive and responsible human being today.

I found her analogy of the securely anonymous person in a cave who is suddenly confronted with the opportunity of becoming an autonomous individual out in the full light of a challenging, frightening, but hope-filled world one of the most perceptive passages in the book. While directed to "women of faith," and challenging religious women who avoid responsibility by expecting God to treat them as puppets, the book speaks to every modern woman as she wrestles with the conflicting demands placed upon her. The "Women's Lib" probably won't like her delineation of some of the tasks women can do best, although she clearly does not close any career to women. The millions of homemakers who are still living in their caves may be stirred to step out and feel the warmth of God's sunshine.

This book can be helpful not only to women, but to educators, counselors, clergymen, husbands, and leaders of voluntary associations who might recruit great numbers of able volunteers if they used the insights here set forth.

CYNTHIA C. WEDEL

Washington, D.C.

PREFACE

The sixties were a decade of dreaming. It began with the presidential victory of Kennedy over Nixon. It was a Man of LeMancha decade with the impossible dream. It was a decade in which the Kennedys shared the dream of Shaw: "Some people see things as they are and say, 'Why?' I dream of things that never were and say, 'Why not?'" And Martin Luther King proclaimed before 250,000 people, "I have a dream!" But the sixties said no to the fulfillment of these dreams—and finally silenced the dreamers. History cycled, and the decade ended with Nixon in the White House.

I believe the seventies must be a decade of innovation, and women must bear their share of the burden. To move beyond feminism is to move beyond imitation, not only of the mistress-madonna image of mass media, but also beyond imitation of the other sex. It is to move from imitation to innovation.

I wonder what would happen if the woman power of the world were unleashed with the intent of creating, out of the chaos of the moment, a future of *arete*—of excellence. A future that would be complementary to the order and magnificence of the

13

universe and to the beauty and diversity of this planet. A future whose possibilities for physical, intellectual, and spiritual growth would match the potentialities of every newborn babe around the globe. Our alternative is passivity, which leads to a lack of will and commitment, to hopelessness and meaninglessness, to helplessness and decay.

This writing deals with reality, as individually perceived; with relatedness, to God through others; and finally with responsibility, as the companion of freedom. I do not write because I have answers; I write in search of solutions. For we gain a deeper and broader consciousness from struggling with the problems. And in this struggle we find hope. For as the sixties showed us the reality of the unfulfilled dream, they also taught us the significance of the search. There is hope, not in the dreams themselves, but in commitment to their innovation. For the future will be not what we *wish* it to be, but what we *shape* it to be.

1

CREATOR AND VICTIM

Recently I went to a ladies' luncheon, held to organize an auxiliary for a day-care center in a low-income area. It was a lovely luncheon. (No one asked for peanut butter and jelly, and there wasn't a single glass of spilled milk!) With unanimous agreement we decided to form the auxiliary. The first item of concern was a monthly meeting day. Thursday was suggested by the steering committee, but this was met with the corporate response: "Not Thursday! That's hairdresser day!"

That evening I went as an observer to a woman's liberation meeting, held to discuss the plight of women in a male supremacist society. It was a lively evening, with everyone in unanimous accord that as women we are discriminated against. The first item of concern was free day-care centers for everyone, staffed by both men and women. The corporate response was affirmative—but nobody wanted to work in one!

As suburban wives and mothers we are stylish, well-educated, and competent—though perhaps a bit superficial, short-sighted, and pampered. As neofeminists we are uninhibited, widely experienced, and intentional—though perhaps a bit ashamed of

15

our sex, constricted, and sometimes crude. In the former group we content ourselves with a busy schedule of luncheons, clubs, and chauffeuring; of hairdresser, supermarket, and shopping center. In the latter group, we expound on our discontent. For we recognize the trap of measuring our worth in terms of clothes, homes, and husbands. But our solution is to call for an end to the nuclear family—as though the phoenix will rise from the ashes. Either way, we consume ourselves in our small spheres— and the planet spins on unchanged.

The rural-oriented image of woman as wife, mother, comforter, nurse, and symbol of virtue placed her on a pedestal and thereby set her out of the way. In this madonna image she was seen as being above, and therefore apart from, the formation of man's social system.

In the fifties and early sixties, this image of woman became urbanized and suburbanized and added another dimension. Mass media sold a chic new image that was consumer-oriented. Woman was seen as spender, tempter, charmer, and perennially young wife. This mistress image portrayed an equally false femininity. Television and magazines sometimes treated her as an overgrown child, excelling in who-has-the-whitest-wash trivia. And many women played the child, which says something about their opinion of their husbands' maturity. Sometimes she was treated as a sex object, a pawn in the Playboy game. And many women allowed themselves to be flaunted and used, which says something about their opinion of themselves. In the mistress image, woman was encouraged toward reliance upon her femaleness rather than toward authentic development and acceptance of responsibility.

And then in the late sixties the mistress-madonna image of woman was called into question. For there were women who wanted to be persons; they wanted to be subjects rather than objects. The neo-feminist rang the bell for a new period in history. And the tinkle became a clang as the liberty bell resounded across the country. But the neo-feminist was seen as a sexless, rebelling, demonstrating antagonist. And in the fury, she blinded herself to the totality of her potentialities, for she hid the qualities attributed to womanhood. Consumed with her self-aggrandizing battle, she forgot to chart her course beyond feminism.

We have fallen victim either to the very comforts and conveniences that should help free us or to the contagious violence and rebellion of the times. Effecting positive change in the world calls for more than imitation of the mistress-madonna image. It also calls for more than imitation of the other sex. It calls for innovative action.

Feminism is concerned with self-actualization for women. For the woman of faith, to move beyond feminism is to be concerned with self-actualization, not as an end in itself, but as a means to effective self-giving. As women, we have intelligence and knowledge. We have the time and money to do what is important to us. We are energetic, capable, and experienced in human relations. What would happen if all this power were called forth and channeled toward creating a world of excellence?

I don't know what the result would be, but I do know we are capable of making an unprecedented impact. A man and his wife were driving to a meeting one night, and he scolded, "For the first time in our marriage, I feel you pulling against me." She just smiled in the darkness, glad that her weight could finally be felt. History has never felt the full force of women's weight in an effort to bend it in a new direction.

There is no place in a world of excellence for overpopulation—but we are the ones who have the babies. No place for starvation—but our country spends more than any other on both food and diet pills, and we are the consumers. No place for urban blight—but the men don't move to the suburbs for the joy of commuting!

To begin to move beyond feminism is to look at our lives and the world from a broader perspective. It is to probe our possibilities. Are we victims or creators—or both? How free are we to shape our own future? How free are we to shape the future of the world? If to some extent we are free, are we also responsible to the same degree?

As human beings we are victims of reality, and, paradoxically, we are also its creators. We have limitations to face. We are thrust i to history at a particular time and place without our consent and then yanked out again before we are ready to leave. We are rational and irrational, progressive and regressive, good and evil. We laugh, and we cry. As we walk through life, we aspire toward beauty—and trip over ugliness. We are queens and clowns, actors and reactors. We advance in hope and retreat in fear. We succeed, and we fail. We are restricted by irreversible biological conditions and by our own self-image. Disasters like the Peruvian earthquake come into being, and a country is shattered and torn apart. Or our own inner lives quake, and as persons we become shattered and fragmented.

Yet we were created with intellect and will, with the desire to love and to be loved, and with the capacity to create new towns in disaster areas and a new life within our own situation. For we are dynamic—capable of changing ourselves and the world. We stand face-to-face with our limitations and push back their boundaries. The ocean held us back, and we conquered it. Then the wilderness, and we tamed it. Now we challenge the confines of earth and reach literally for the stars. We plan our families and lengthen our life-span. We heal the previously incurable and dare to suggest we can defy death through freezing. For the first time in history we can intentionally determine our own evolution. We are not helplessly bound by our limitations. To face reality is to acknowledge that at the same time we are victims whose lives are restricted, we are also creators who live in freedom.

The determinists would have us believe that freedom is a farce, that we have no freedom. For example, Freud tells us we are not free: we are victims of our past. Everything wrong is the fault of our parents. Some years ago I heard a story about a mother who was as concerned about her baby's psychological development as she was about his physical progress. She took him to a renowned psychiatrist, who looked at the baby and asked, "How old is he?"

"Six weeks," she replied.

"It's too late!" sentenced the psychiatrist.

The behaviorists tell us we are not free: we are victims of the stimuli surrounding us—like the rats in their experiments.

Our scientific age tells us we are not free: we are victims of the powerful destructive forces we have created. We create the means to annihilation, and yet as individuals stand helpless and powerless before these means.

And there are those who, in the name of religion, tell us we are not free: we are victims of God. They envision God as a cosmic puppeteer, and we are mere puppets whose strings he pulls.

Ironically, even in the deterministic view, regardless of its source, there is a certain amount of freedom. For one does not have to accept responsibility for the consequences of his actions. It releases him from having to think through the issues that arise in his daily living. He can be sure of himself and charge ahead—for whatever will be will be. Being released from responsibility, he bears no guilt. He looks at the mess the world is in and blames it on God—or some other determining factor.

I cannot do this. I do not believe that we are simply products of our past, or responders to stimuli, or robots of our scientific creations, nor pawns in a cosmic chess game. A belief in determinism undermines our sense of responsibility and our ability to commit ourselves. We become convinced that our actions can do no good, that our commitment is to no avail. This affects us inwardly—spiritually. God, in his total love, created us as free and entrusted his world to our keeping. We are free to ignore this or to respond to his love by accepting responsibility for his world. Our response is not a verbal yes or no, or a committed facade. Whether we accept or reject our responsibility for the world is evidenced through our total life style. It includes the effort we exert to reach our own potential; how we use our time and money; the things to which we are committed and the quality of our struggle toward these commitments; how we treat other people; and the way we care for our natural resources and involve ourselves in patterning society.

If we consider ourselves determined, naturally or supernaturally, we simply resign our lives to forces beyond our control and upon which we are dependent. We see ourselves as helpless, and we paralyze our potentiality. We become utterly victimized— not by external forces, but by our own perceptions.

I have a friend whose name is David. He is an outstanding leader in his community. He is also responsibly involved in his church. In high school he was voted the all-around boy and elected president of his class. He was a first-rate football player on his high school team—until he was stricken with polio. He lay on the hospital bed with both legs paralyzed and agonized from the very depths of his being: "Oh, God!" But the situation did not change. No "Be healed!" thundered through the cosmos. David heard nothing, and he saw nothing. But in the silence God said, "Live your life." And David heard. He struggled between victim and creator. He took hold of his situation, and within it he began to create his future. His life is a response to God's love—for it is a life of service. He assumes responsibility, not only for his own life, but also for the lives of those around him. David's legs are still paralyzed, but he is not a victim; he is a *free* man.

If we are free, we are also responsible. We have no scapegoats. If we are free to reach toward our potentialities, to create our own lives, and to shape our society, then we are also responsible for the potentiality we reach, for the life we create, and for the society we shape. Robert Hamill, in *How Free Are You?* states: "The freedom of the Christian man is the freedom to be what God intends him to be, by delivering him out of every little bondage into a great purpose that he can freely serve." [1] If we are to create a world of excellence, one of our tasks is to freely serve.

God has thrust us into the pre-twenty-first century. We stand in the present—in the *now*—with all its evils, all its confusions, all its possibilities. We live in a time of overpopulation, urban blight, polarization, starvation, pollution, senseless war. But we are free to determine our stance toward these conditions.

Our tragic dimensions are not our various limitations and situations in themselves; it is how we relate to these realities that causes or prevents tragedy. In Greek drama the horror always occurred offstage. The focal point was not the horror, but the meaning

[1] (Nashville: Abingdon Press, 1956), p. 60.

22

of the horror. Viktor Frankl, an existential psycho-
therapist, points out that "everything can be taken
from a man but one thing: the last of the human
freedoms—to choose one's attitude in any given set
of circumstances, to choose one's own way." [2] Crises
exist—both world and personal—and either we are
hopelessly victimized or we become creative within
them. To become creative within a situation does
not necessarily mean to find a solution. In our
achievement-oriented society we are in the habit of
measuring success by accomplishment rather than
effort. We prefer to attain small "quickie" goals
rather than to struggle toward impossible vital ones.
But today's problems are too complex to have simple
answers. To become creative in our chaotic world
means that we search for a better way, that we enter
the unending struggle to build more meaningful
lives and a more fully human world.

Sometimes we are so overwhelmed by the chaos
around us that we see ourselves only as victims of
the present, and not as creators of the future. We
shrink from the present. Instead of walking straight-
forwardly into the future, we turn around and see
only the past. We revel in its glories, nostalgic for
that day gone by. We long for stability and certainty, for the good old days of the small town with
its sidewalks lined with trees, when somehow time
seemed to go more slowly, and years went by with
little change. Yards were bigger then, and friends
grew older instead of moving away, and there was
no threat of annihilation. We yearn for the quiet

[2] *From Death-Camp to Existentialism,* trans. Ilse Lasch
(Boston: Beacon Press, 1959), p. 65.

23

frame church at the village center, where babies were baptized and later confirmed, then their weddings celebrated, and finally death's separation shared. We are like Foxy Whitman in *Couples*, whose childhood images "had vanished everywhere but in [her] heart. She went to church to salvage something." [3]

But the church that is simply a salvage yard is not the faithful Body of Christ. For it stands still; it sacrifices faith for security. It ignores the reality of the present. Thomas Wolfe catches this in *Look Homeward, Angel:* Leonard, who had to withdraw from the Methodist Church because of his remarks on Darwin's theory, was "an example of that sad liberalism of the village—an advanced thinker among the Methodists, a bearer of the torch at noon, an apologist for the toleration of ideas that have been established for fifty years." [4] It is because of fear that the church sacrifices the Leonards.

When I was a little girl, I liked to draw houses. I always included flowers and trees, and curtains at the windows. Recently my son Dirk drew a picture of a house in much the same way, with flowers and trees and curtains—but there in the background was Apollo XI on its way to the moon! The present is not like the past. But if we are to be faithful members of the Body of Christ, it is our task to live the Word in the present. To do so is to stand with courage and faith, accepting the radical reality of the moment.

[3] John Updike, *Couples* (New York: Alfred A. Knopf, 1968), p. 42.

[4] (New York: Charles Scribner's Sons, 1929), pp. 232-33.

Frankl tells us that once potentialities are actualized, "they are rendered realities at that very moment, they are saved and delivered into the past, wherein they are rescued and preserved from transitoriness. For in the past, nothing is irrevocably lost, but everything is irrevocably stored." [5] But potentialities which are not chosen are lost. The future with all its possibilities pushes in upon us, falling on the foundation of the past. As we select and discard the various possibilities available to us, we create our own futures. To move in one direction is to enhance future possibilities along that course. But at the same time it is to decide not to go in the other direction, which delimits it and all the possibilities it would have opened. The future keeps pouring in upon us, and we keep moving along—opening certain doors—and thus automatically closing others. And oftentimes we are not even aware a decision has been made!

We need to become conscious of these decisions in our everyday lives. Sartre has a word for us here that we cannot ignore: "Man first exists . . . hurls himself toward a future . . . conscious of imagining himself . . . in the future. . . . Man will be what he will have planned to be. Not what he will want to be." [6] Ouch! My planning stands like a pygmy beside the giant of my wanting. I do not like to think in terms of a step-by-step struggle, of my actions today having consequences that limit or enhance my

[5] *Man's Search for Meaning*, trans. Ilse Lasch (Boston: Beacon Press, 1962), p. 122.

[6] *Existentialism*, trans. Bernard Frectman (New York: Philosophical Library, 1947), pp. 18-19.

future possibilities. It makes today's acts so important. I'd rather think in terms of Santa Claus or Superman or a hocus-pocus of some sort to transport me magically from where I am to where I want to be.

Reinzi, in *Daughter of Silence*, grasps the significance of consequences: "This was the tragedy of the human condition: that every single act was contingent upon another in the past and spawned a litter of consequences for the future. . . . The consequences spread out, ripples in a limitless pool, currents eternally moving in a dark sea." [7] But this human condition is not doomed to result in tragedy. For if the negative causes ripples, so does the positive. Every time we touch one who is lonely, feed one who is hungry, provide a coat for one who is cold and a cool drink for one who is hot, every time we smile at one who scowls, understand the insecurity of one who boasts, affirm the worth of one who feels worthless, and reach for humanness in the inhuman—every time, we send ripples, perhaps waves, into the sea of the future.

Life is God's gift. It is not to be feared but accepted—as it is, with all its limitations and all its freedom. It is to be explored and shared and known and felt. It is to be *lived*. It is to be lived *now*, for time is going by. The earth rotates, and the sun rises and sets, rises and sets, marking off our lives.

Kazantzakis tells a story of an old man looking

[7] Morris West, *Daughter of Silence* (New York: William Morrow and Company, 1961), p. 42.

into a brook with deep concentration.[8] A priest approaches and leans over to see what holds the old man's attention—but sees nothing except the water.

"What are you looking at, grandfather?"

The old man raises his head and smiles sadly. "At my life flowing and disappearing, son, flowing and disappearing."

"Don't worry, grandfather, it knows where it's going—toward the sea, everyone's life flows toward the sea."

The old man sighs. "Yes, my son, that is why the sea is salty—from the many tears."

Our lives flow and disappear; flow and disappear. Time moves on, and each moment is rendered into the past.

Once at a women's meeting the speaker advised us: "When you hit thirty, you need to learn how to do something new each year because you can't depend on your face and figure anymore." I was all of twenty-one. But I blinked my eyes only a couple of times—and now her words apply to me. I feel like Jess in *Except for Me and Thee*, when he asks his wife:

"Thee glad to have it summer, Eliza?"
"Summer for us, too," she said unexpectedly.
"Summer," Jess repeated, startled. Said that way, the word shook him. He felt himself no more than started in life, a few steps taken on a journey of miles. . . . They had come to a halfway mark.[9]

[8] Nikos Kazantzakis, *The Fratricides*, trans. Athena Gianakas Dallas (New York: Simon and Schuster, 1964), p. 17.
[9] Jessamyn West, *Except for Me and Thee* (New York: Harcourt, Brace & World, 1969), p. 73.

So soon we reach the summer of life. Where did the time go? We are somehow numbed to the content of the moment—and then later suddenly startled by the reality that much has happened without our awareness. We seem oblivious to our present—our *now*—until it is past. And then it is too late.

The past is behind us. It is irreversible. The present is upon us. Frankl suggests that "we pretend we are at the end of our lives, reviewing our own biography, and as we come to the chapter dealing with the present phase of our lives we have the power to decide what the contents of the next chapter shall be." [10] We are writing that chapter now. It includes certain limitations. It includes the manner in which we relate to these limitations. The blank pages will be filled with a tale of tragedy whose heroine is a victim. Or we can fill them with a story of one who tries in the spirit of Christ to create within her limitations the possibilities for a better world in the future.

My grandmother, who is in her eighties, watched the first moon landing with us. As Armstrong set his foot on the moon, she glanced at her past: "I came to Oklahoma in a covered wagon. I've known the first car, the first silent movie, the first talkie, the first radio, telephone, TV, colored TV, airplane, jet, rocket, and now the first moon landing. What a time to live a life!"

Yes, what a time to *live* a life! What a time to freely serve! What a time to begin to create a future of excellence!

[10] *The Doctor and the Soul* (New York: Alfred A. Knopf, 1955), p. 73.

2

THE CHALLENGE OF
RESPONSIBILITY

One evening, after busying themselves for a long
while behind a closed door with a sign marked
"Keep Out," our children presented Bill and me
with several pictures. "The flowers are for you,
Mother, because you like pretty flowers. Here, Daddy, the mountains are for you. They're big, and you
like to fish." The differences that children see between their mothers and fathers are acted out in
their play, and they learn the masculine and feminine characteristics. The biological differences and
the cultural influences combine so that role expectations differ for the man and the woman. There is
disagreement about the extent to which these characteristics are innate or learned. It seems to me,
however, that the important factor is that they do
exist.

We are in the midst of a movement toward
greater overlapping of masculine-feminine roles.
Traditional structures are being called into question,
and whenever this happens we are frightened, because we are not secure with the new and unfamiliar.
We may not be comfortable with the old structures,
but we are even less comfortable with the uncer-

tainty of what change will bring. We are aware that the requirements of a housewife in the pre–twenty-first century are quite different from those in past generations. Technology has eased our labor and increased our leisure. Machines have broken the bonds that tied us to endless life-consuming household duties. There is no longer justification for the lifelong solitary role of housewife for woman. To pretend otherwise is to delude ourselves. This is threatening—for being a housewife has been our noble all-encompassing role since Eve.

As a result, a polarization has occurred between those who would do away with the nuclear family completely and those who would limit themselves entirely to serving it—between those who would absorb the traditional feminine role into the masculine one and those who would continue it per se.

And caught in the middle will be found the bright and sensitive woman who recognizes the importance of the feminine role, but simultaneously questions the authenticity of the mistress-madonna image. She wants to be somebody's wife and somebody's mother, but she wants also to be who she is: a person in her own right. She wants the freedom to actualize her perceived potential rather than to live vicariously through her husband and children. She feels her responsibility to society includes, but also reaches beyond, caring for her immediate family.

When John F. Kennedy appointed the Commission on the Status of Women, he said: "We have by no means done enough to strengthen family life and at the same time encourage women to make their full contribution as citizens." [1] If masculine-feminine roles are broadly based and flexible rather than narrow and rigid, persons can cooperate on the basis of interest and competency. A free interchange not only allows an open-ended pursuit of one's perceived potential, but it also removes a barrier to society's optimum development. This means that both masculine and feminine roles are broadened and to a greater degree overlap. It does not mean a feminine eclipse—a hiding of the feminine role.

Some psychologists have attributed men with achievement motivation and women with affiliation motivation. They suggest that whereas a man's occupation is the basis for his status, a woman's husband is the basis for her status. With regard to "life chances," her choice of husband functions like a man's choice of occupation.[2] However, the strength of the neo-feminists would indicate a current movement toward achievement motivation in women also.

The National Organization of Women (NOW), under the leadership of Betty Friedan, is attempting to deal with the obstacles to woman's achievement in the working world. It battles against discrimination in salary and promotion and also points to the need for return-guaranteed paid maternity leave, as

[1] *American Women*, Report of the President's Commission on the Status of Women, 1963, p. 1.

[2] Barrie Stacey, "Achievement Motivation, Occupational Choice and Inter-Generation Occupational Mobility," *Human Relations*, XXII (June, 1969), 275-81.

well as government-supported child-care centers.

Other groups in the women's liberation movement are more radical than NOW. They question the validity of the nuclear family and blame it for keeping women in an inferior position. They call for an end to the myths of woman's passivity and her physical and intellectual inferiority. They demand total freedom and equality, and with the goal of adequate physical education for women, especially in self-defense, they are prepared to fight! These women refuse to submerge their perceived potential in the traditionally subordinate place of woman. They call us to first-class citizenship and to be *all* that we are capable of being as persons. This is a summons that needs to be heard.

But another thought must be interjected: a woman cannot be *all* she is capable of being if she rejects her space in the whole; for as part of the whole, she transcends herself—as does man. Paul Tillich points out that self-affirmation and commitment beyond the self, which seem to be contradictory requirements, are most nearly resolved when we see ourselves reflecting a larger harmony, as bearers of the creative process of the universe, as microcosmic participants in the creative processes of the macrocosm.[3] There is an ecological niche for the feminine role which, if left unfilled, leaves a void in our social system.

It seems to me that we need a model for women which encourages a mother to make her contribution to society beyond the home, but at the same

[3] *The Courage to Be* (New Haven: Yale University Press, 1952), p. 52.

time takes seriously the needs of her family. Neither being the victim of a full-time mother who is distraught and neurotic nor competing for attention in a day nursery is conducive to a child's optimum development.

One morning a little child at a day-care center picked a wild flower to present to his mother. The worker had too many children to bother putting it in water, so the little boy put it in his pocket. During the five o'clock rush when the mothers came for their children, he was waiting eagerly by the door with his gift in his hand. But a little girl bumped his arm, and he dropped it. Before he could pick it up, a little boy stepped on it. When his mother arrived, she was tired from her day, harried from the traffic, and felt rushed to get home to cook dinner. He offered her his precious symbol of love, but she saw only a smashed wilted weed and received the gift accordingly. The child learned that the giving of himself is meaningless.

Erik Erikson states: "The future of mankind may well depend on the fate of a 'mother variable' uncontrolled by technological man." [4] The time of preschool children can be a precious stage in the life of both the mother and the child. All mothers and their children share love, but the full-time mother and preschool child offer each other the rare gift of leisure. If a woman has thought through her life cycle, she knows that this stage is relatively brief, and she can relish the joys it offers. There will be time enough in the next stage for competitive-

[4] *Insight and Responsibility* (New York: W. W. Norton, 1964), p. 235.

33

ness and confrontation of social structures. This is a time for gentle caring. It is a time for the little kindnesses so often lost in urbanization—taking food when there is illness or death, being thoughtful of another person, or simply remembering a birthday. It is a time for sewing and decoupage. It is a time for exchanging recipes and planting flowers and sitting in the sun. It is a time for taking walks in the spring and having lunch in the park with other mothers and their children. It is a marvelous stage, and if we are to be responsible, we cannot ignore it—but neither can we drag it out until our "babies" have their own babies!

We have developed humanistic qualities in caring for our families that need to be channeled into society. Myron Brenton suggests:

It cannot be denied that a woman's upbringing and her deep involvement in child care activities lead her to develop to a greater degree humanistic traits like sympathy, understanding, and patience, and that the male's struggle in the competitive arena leads him to develop to a greater degree other traits, which give him the strongest supports in meeting the demands of his particular challenges.[5]

We cannot pretend, as some of the neo-feminists seem to, that these traits are unimportant, but neither can we pretend that our sex excuses us from responsibility for the world. To take seriously the task of channeling our humanistic qualities into society requires knowledge of societal needs and of

[5] *The American Male* (New York: Coward-McCann, 1966), pp. 223-24.

our individual abilities and interests; it also requires conscious decisions with regard for the amount of time we can spend outside the home in the various stages of our lives, for our financial freedom, and for the void in society we can most effectively fill.

This calls into question the value of taking a meaningless job—without economic necessity— simply for the sake of getting out of the house. Why nine-to-five-it punching a typewriter instead of a stove, or folding letters instead of clothes, or filing cards instead of recipes? Gilbert Chesterson quipped on the emancipation of women: "Twenty million young women rose to their feet with the cry, 'We will not be dictated to,' and promptly became stenographers." [6] On the other hand, of course, women can club and coffee their lives away. There is more to the living of life than either of these allows. If the unemployed woman is intentional about her use of time, she can channel her leisure not only toward the actualization of her perceived potential, but also toward benefiting society through meaningful and important volunteer work. In the same way, the employed woman's job can be a means of self-expression and of benefit to society.

Remuneration neither increases nor lessens the significance of a task that needs to be done. If I may generalize, the volunteer has a tendency to feel a bit self-righteous, just as the salaried woman is inclined a bit toward smugness about her ability to hold a

[6] Cited in "Women in a New Age: Selected Materials from the National Seminar of the Woman's Division of Christian Service" (Cincinnati, Ohio: Board of Missions Service Center, The Methodist Church, 1964), pp. 30-31.

job *and* run a house. Yet, the latter knows the guilt of less involvement with her children, and the former is somewhat threatened by the phrase "just a housewife." But if we are assured of our significance, of our uniqueness and place in the whole, we do not measure our worth by a paycheck. We can find the kinds of jobs that fit our interests and abilities and then choose between the paid and unpaid ones on the basis of our financial situations and desires. We do not have to earn money to prove our worth— nor avoid it to prove the worth of our husbands.

When we talk of giving ourselves away to create a world of excellence, we are not talking about simply responding to every request laid upon us. Nor are we discussing licking envelopes or collecting donations—though these things need to be done. Effective self-giving is much more complex. We are talking about the deliberate, intentional, studied channel of service that a woman chooses. It requires a knowledge of one's abilities, information about the needs in the particular area being considered, and a period of preparation to become qualified to do the work well. This is true whether we are considering a paid or a significant volunteer position. John W. Gardner suggests that "everyone, either in his career or as a part-time activity, should be doing *something* about which he cares deeply." [7] Every woman needs to do something that calls forth her potentiality and allows her to be involved in a way that she finds meaningful.

[7] *Self-Renewal: The Individual and the Innovative Society* (New York: Harper Colophon edition, Harper and Row, 1965), pp. 16-17.

One of the reasons for our frustration over what to do with ourselves is the lack of available and comprehensive programs of career development especially designed for women. If we have been exposed to career development at all, the program was probably geared to men. There are several differentiations between the life patterns of men and those of married women. After her children were grown, a forty-five-year-old woman wanted to go back to college and become a school counselor. The academic advisor discouraged her, "You're too old. It takes too long." But she had *twenty years* left before retirement. Why not spend them training for what she wanted to do and then do it as long as she could? She, and women like her, who want to look forward instead of backward, bring with them the rare combination of the person-centered qualities they have developed, the wisdom of their years, and a fresh enthusiasm for their jobs. This combination can make them valuable assets in their fields. One of the vital needs in our changing world is a program of career development which takes seriously both a woman's desire to actualize her perceived potential and her roles of wife and mother.

In the first place, career development for women should recognize our development of humanistic qualities. We need an opportunity to learn how to effectively channel these attributes into areas of our society where they are most needed.

A second criterion should be our interrupted work history. We need work schedules that correspond with school hours and vacations. Government service could provide mothers' schedules, which would

37

be mutually beneficial. Education could use part-time teachers, which would help fill the teacher shortage as well as provide a mother with an opportunity to contribute her abilities.

Thirdly, volunteer work should be an aspect of our career development. One of the major ways we influence our communities is through significant positions as volunteers.

Finally, our lengthening life-span must be considered. Today's married couples have an average of fifteen years to share together after their youngest child is grown up and gone.[8] In 1900 the *life expectancy* of an American woman was forty-eight years; now the *average age* of the working woman is forty-one. More than half a million women are eighty-five or over. In these lonely later years we will benefit from a well-established habit of being involved in something that we find meaningful.

Our educational systems lag in this area, partially because career development for women is relatively new. But the reason for the lag is also that we have generally left major educational planning to the men, and they are not as aware of this need as we are. One of our contributions as women can be to expand the availability of career development for women. Learning how to give ourselves responsibly at the different stages in our lives is a must if we are to create a world of excellence.

Women basically fall into two broad categories. One of these is composed of the women discussed in the preceding pages who do not have to earn

[8] *American Women*, p. 66.

money. They become employed or accept volunteer positions as a means to self-actualization and self-giving. The second group is made up of women who must work. These are the single, divorced, and widowed, as well as the married whose earnings are needed to help support their families. The category in which a woman finds herself, as well as her educational level and experience within it, will largely determine her freedom to choose a position that is meaningful to her and of benefit to society.

The women who work because of economic necessity are sometimes forgotten in our prosperous society. Regardless of the kind of job they hold or the salary they earn, they are confronted with difficulties that arise because of their sex. They face problems of prejudice, fair wages, child care, and family life. But their problems oftentimes get lost in our eagerness to say a word pro or con about the women who are free to choose whether or not to work.

The problem of prejudice is best evidenced in the life of the single woman who tries to make a place for herself that matches her interests and abilities. She commits herself to a particular profession, is trained for it, and becomes experienced in it. She is not geographically dependent upon a husband and does not interrupt her career for birth and child-rearing. Without family concerns and financial worries to fragment her, she can zero in on her profession with alertness and lucidity. She has ample time for continuing study. There is nothing to deter her from success in her field—except her sex.

This prejudice is as strong among women as it is among men. Those of us who are dependent upon our husbands for a living do not want some woman competing with him for promotions. And the men certainly do not welcome her! Perhaps this is why the single woman who has a full and meaningful life can still hear society whispering, "Isn't it a pity she didn't marry?" The contrast between "bachelor" and "old maid" is not very flattering to womankind. Tradition seems not to have recognized that an unmarried woman is as fully a person as an unmarried man.

Our culture has taught us that success in competition with men is unfeminine. A study conducted by Matina S. Horner concluded that women have a will to fail, that we will feign failure rather than successfully compete with men.[9] This attitude is not very complimentary to men, for it implies that their competency is based on our artificial incompetency. Both sexes need to recognize that what men are is not dependent upon what women are not. Brenton suggests:

The ultimate masculine challenge . . . does away with stereotypes, guidelines, and life plans. It simply requires a man to be more fully human, more fully responsive, and more fully functioning than he has ever before allowed himself to be. This is the freedom that equality of the sexes offers him.[10]

If men and women are successful in this new approach, both our children and our society will have broader opportunities for optimum development.

One of the benefits of woman's broadened re-

[9] "Woman's Will to Fail," *Psychology Today*, III (November, 1969), 36-38.
[10] *The American Male*, p. 233.

sponsibility is its effect on the lives of children. At the dinner table Mom has a contribution to make—much more interesting than the neighborhood gossip or complaints about being *exhausted* from picking up after the family. She can add to their knowledge of the community, its adequacies and inadequacies. The children profit from an opportunity to grow up in an atmosphere in which social responsibility is assumed. As little girls identify with their mothers, they are offered a new model. They do not only see care for the family, but also self-discipline, intentional use of time, and community action, which provide an opportunity for them to develop broader-based self-expectations. Mom's contribution also helps little boys move beyond the myth of the patriarchal family.

In our culture the feminine role offers a sensitivity and tenderness, a leisure time for caring for others. It is a healthy balance to the competitive and aggressive male forces. A problem exists of equalizing the significance of the roles without simply absorbing the feminine role into the masculine one—which seems to be the current trend. Perhaps a solution is broadening the feminine role, so that a woman's care is not limited to her own family and home, but is spread to her community.

Today's young American woman comes to maturity with a special measure of opportunity—to live in a period when American abundance is coupled with a quest for quality, to show forth excellence in her life as an individual, to transmit a desire for it to her children, and to help make it evident in her community.[11]

The patterns of society are made by men and women—whether by direct action or default. Leadership is needed from both sexes, and both have a responsibility to contribute fully.

[11] *American Women*, p. 71.

3

THE STRUGGLE FOR FREEDOM

The freedom to shape society is relatively new in woman's history. Though Jesus lifted the status of women from their subordination in the Old Testament, the church fathers generally leaned on Paul for woman's proper (and lowly) place. But even he admitted: "There is neither Jew nor Greek, there is neither bond nor free, there is neither male nor female: for ye are all one in Christ Jesus" (Galatians 3:28). Both inside the church and outside it, we have been struggling for centuries to actualize our equality with men.

Feminism as a world movement usually dates from 1792, when Mary Wollstonecraft, in *Vindication of the Rights of Women*, denounced the idea that we exist only to please men. In America, it officially began with the first woman's rights convention in Seneca Falls, New York, in 1848. The leaders were Elizabeth Cady Stanton, Lucretia Mott, Martha Wright, and Mary Ann McClintock. With a political finesse that is a tribute to womanhood, they clothed their Declaration of Sentiments in the magnificent language of the Declaration of Independence.[1] At that time one of the arguments against equality was that women were weak and needed special protection. Sojourner Truth, a Negro freed-woman, responded to this at a woman's rights convention in Akron, Ohio, in 1851:

Nobody ever helps me into carriages or over puddles, or gives me the best place—and ain't I a woman? . . . I have ploughed and planted and gathered into barns . . . and ain't I a woman? . . . I have borne thirteen children, and seen most of 'em sold into slavery, and when I cried out with my mother's grief none but Jesus heard me—and ain't I a woman? [2]

The weaker sex has struggled forcefully for suffrage, education, and employment. Not all women, of course, have wanted these dimensions of freedom —just as not all men have opposed them. And when freedom has been gained, it has not always been used responsibly—by men or women. To glimpse the struggle is to become proud of the foundation upon which we stand and to celebrate the vision of these futuric women of the past.

THE DIMENSION OF SUFFRAGE

In 1776, Abigail Adams wrote to her husband John, who was sitting with the Continental Congress:

[1] *Victory: How Women Won It*. A Centennial Symposium by the National American Woman Suffrage Association (New York: The H. W. Wilson Company, 1940), pp. 24-27.

[2] Caroline Bird, *Born Female: The High Cost of Keeping Women Down* (New York: David McKay Company, 1968), p. 31.

I long to hear you have declared an independency, and, by the way, in the new code of laws which I suppose it will be necessary to make, I desire you would remember the ladies and be more favorable to them than your ancestors. . . . If particular care and attention are not paid to the ladies, we are determined to foment a rebellion and will not hold ourselves bound to obey any laws in which we have no voice or representation.[3]

But 150 years passed before men actualized the equality of women to have a voice in government.

That century and a half was filled with ups and downs. New Jersey's constitution of 1776—two days before independence was declared—granted taxpaying women the vote, but this right was retracted in 1807, with the explanation that, although "qualified women had used the vote quite generally, they had not supported the right candidates in the election"![4] The earliest lasting woman's suffrage in history was passed in the territory of Wyoming in 1869. In spite of this first, twenty-six countries granted the right to vote to women before the United States.[5] The Federal Amendment for Woman Suffrage, first introduced in the Senate in 1878, was passed in 1919—forty-one years later. Ratification was needed by thirty-six states.

Throughout the suffrage campaign, man dutifully warned woman of the consequences of going to the polls: she would become harsh and competitive,

[3] Carrie Chapman Catt and Nettie Rogers Shuler, *Woman Suffrage and Politics* (New York: Charles Scribner's Sons, 1926), pp. 8-9.

[4] *Ibid.*, p. 9.

[5] *Ibid.*, p. viii.

lose the chivalrous deference of men, and ruin her health by going to vote in bad weather and over poor roads.[6] This prophesied degradation brought mock horror from Alice Duer Miller, who wrote a poem in which a mother talks to her son on his twenty-first birthday:

> You must not go to the polls, Willie,
> Never go to the polls,
> They're dark and dreadful places
> Where many lose their souls;
> They smirch, degrade and coarsen,
> Terrible things they do
> To quiet, elderly women—
> What would they do to you! [7]

But not all was humorous. The suffragists had to contend with ignorance and prejudice on the part of public officials. An example is the written statement of a state senator of Wisconsin (quoted verbatim):

Why I Voted against Women Suff
I I an my Wife agree on point I, a hous Wife belongs to home near her children and to keep hous, and not in open public Politic.
2ond. it is only for the city Women in larger Cities that want to vote and to get the controll of the Country vote. to Elect State officers and President of the U.S. because a Country Women wont not go to Vote they

[6] Thomas Woody, A History of Women's Education in the United States (New York: The Science Press, 1929), II: 444.

[7] From the book Are Women People? by Alice Duer Miller. Copyright 1914 by George H. Doran Company. Reprinted by permission of Doubleday & Company, Inc.

have all they wont to do to take care of their children
and House Work garden and etc.
3th a Danger that the men will not go to the poles if
the Women get Elected to any state Legislature. the
big Danger will be that some hair pulling will going on
if there will be Women Elected in the State Legislature
they will be worse as the Attorneys at present.[8]

Despite all this reasonable and literate opposition,
the women prevailed! The first two states to ratify
the nineteenth amendment were Illinois and Wisconsin; the thirty-sixth was Tennessee.

The suffrage struggle came to an end, and we had
a new dimension of freedom. The National American Woman Suffrage Association held a victory
convention in Chicago, and the League of Women
Voters was born. This organization has often been
futuric in its concerns. For example, pollution has
recently become a major national issue, but the
League began to study water pollution back in the
fifties. It continues today as a nonpartisan group of
women seeking to be informed themselves and to
inform others. The League of Women Voters is a
symbol of woman's attempt to use the hard-won
freedom of suffrage responsibly.

THE DIMENSION OF EDUCATION

In the eighteenth century, Jean Jâcques Rousseau
stated: "The whole of education of women ought

[8] Wisconsin *State Journal*, June 22, 1919. Senator Herman
Bilgrien, fearful that the press would misquote him, carefully
wrote out his statement. Cited in Catt and Shuler, *Woman
Suffrage and Politics*, p. 345.

to be relative to men, to please them, to educate them when young, to care for them when grown, to counsel them, and to make life sweet and agreeable to them." [9] At that time the goal of education for women had nothing to do with personal potentiality.

In early America, the dame schools, which taught four- to seven-year-olds to read and write, were the only niche in education filled by woman teachers. Girls could attend, but they were usually taught to read only a little and not to write at all, for "they might forge their husbands' signatures." [10]

Despite unequal opportunities, some girls excelled scholastically. One of these was Lucinda Foote, who studied with her brothers who were preparing for Yale. In 1783, at the age of twelve, she was examined and declared "fully qualified, except in regard to sex, to be received as a pupil of the Freshman class of Yale University." [11] She and women like her not only provided leadership during the secondary education movement, but proved that women were capable of higher learning.

In 1836—*two hundred years* after the founding of Harvard (the first college in America)—the Georgia Female College was chartered. A year later, Oberlin College in Ohio ushered in collegiate coedu-

[9] *Émile or Treatise on Education*, trans. William H. Payne (New York: D. Appleton, 1918), p. 263.

[10] Mabel Newcomer, *A Century of Higher Education for American Women* (New York: Harper & Brothers, 1959), p. 7.

[11] Woody, *History of Women's Education*, II: 137.

cation by enrolling four women. Three of them received the A.B. degree in 1841—the first undisputed instance in this country of women receiving bachelor's degrees equal to those granted to men.[12] Coeducation became the mode for the land-grant colleges and state universities, with the University of Iowa leading the way in 1855. By the 1930's, two in five B.A.'s and M.A.'s and one in seven Ph.D.'s were conferred upon women. By the 1960's, however, this ratio had decreased to one in three B.A.'s and M.A.'s and one in ten Ph.D.'s.[13]

The fear that educated women would make incompetent—and probably bored—housewives is illustrated in the following conversation between a father and his daughter:

"I have made 100 in algebra, 96 in Latin, 90 in Greek, 88½ in mental philosophy and 95 in history; are you not satisfied with my record?"

To which the father replied: "Yes, indeed, and if your husband happens to know anything about housekeeping, sewing and cooking, I am sure your married life will be very happy." [14]

In 1891 the trustees of Randolph Macon aspired to reconcile education with feminine attributes by establishing a college "where the dignity and strength of fully-developed faculties and the charm of the highest literary culture may be acquired by our daughters without loss to woman's crowning glory—

[12] Newcomer, *A Century of Higher Education*, p. 5.
[13] *American Women*, p. 11.
[14] Woody, *History of Women's Education*, II: 52.

her gentleness and grace." [15] So it would seem that the goal of equal education was not that women might become the same as men, but that they might reach their potentialities as persons.

THE DIMENSION OF EMPLOYMENT

The first American poet was a woman, Mrs. Anne Bradstreet, who was born in the seventeenth century. In reflecting upon the male view of women in her day, she concluded a verse:

> For such despite they cast on female wits,
> If what I do prove well, it won't advance—
> They'll say it's stolen, or else it was by chance. [16]

It appears that men in this country have always been prejudiced against women's success in non-domestic areas!

According to Elisabeth Dexter, colonial women had a greater amount of freedom in work than those of the nineteenth century. It was common for a woman to help her husband in his business, and the single and widowed were encouraged to support themselves and their families however they could. [17] Women were among the printers, authors, innkeepers, shopkeepers, and, though rarely, landowners.

---

[15] Frederick Rudolph, *The American College and University* (New York: Vintage Books, 1962), p. 329.

[16] *Poems With her Prose Remains* (New York: 1897), p. 8.

[17] *Colonial Women of Affairs: Women in Business and the Professions in America Before 1776* (Boston: Houghton Mifflin Company, 1931), pp. 181 ff.

The were also engaged as actresses and craftswomen. They acted as administrators and executors, and were given power of attorney. Medical careers were restricted, but until the nineteenth century, women had a legal monopoly as midwives. This occupational openness was partially due to the Puritan work ethic. It was also a matter of practicality; for there was so much work to be done in this new land that it just did not matter who did it.

Since the men needed all the help they could get, slave trade prospered. On a slaver that arrived in Boston in 1761 was a frail little girl who became one of the notable women of the eighteenth century: Phillis Wheatley, the first Black poetess. The highlight of her career was her short stay in London, where she was greatly honored and would have been presented at court if she had not returned to America to care for her mistress who was fatally ill. One of George Washington's letters, dated February 28, 1776, is written to her and concludes:

If you should ever come to Cambridge, or near headquarters, I shall be happy to see a person so favored by the Muses, to whom nature has been so liberal and beneficent in her dispensations. I am, with great respect, your obedient humble servant.[18]

Soon after, she was freed by the death of her master.

Within a few decades, women began to respond to the cruel dehumanization of the Blacks. In fact,

[18] Jared Sparks, *The Writings of George Washington; Being His Correspondence, Addresses, Messages, and Other Papers, Official and Private, Selected and Published from the Original Manuscripts*, III (Boston: Ferdinand Andrews, Publisher, 1840), pp. 297-98.

slavery was the first political question that women made an effort to affect. They organized the National Female Anti-Slavery Society in 1833.[19] Many of its members included Phillis Wheatley's poetry in their reading. Perhaps some of them were spurred to act on the Negro's behalf by the poignant image of this frail poet, scrubbing boardinghouse floors until her strength broke, and dying without food for her baby or wood to warm her room. For in the deprivation of the post-Revolutionary War years, as in the financial crisis of this century, the difficulties were compounded for the Blacks.

The Civil War was one of the events that weakened the sex barrier to employment that had developed by the nineteenth century. It caused a shortage of men, and women filled many of the empty places on the men's labor force. The other event was the Industrial Revolution. Though manufacturing was almost entirely limited to the household, prior to the beginning of the nineteenth century, the factory system was dominant by mid-century. Women were common as employees—but not as employers. The widows and orphans who worked in the factories were the victims of inhuman treatment and horrible working conditions.

Again women responded. Some of them were social workers who had been graduated from the new women's colleges.[20] These women—some of them wives of the men responsible—strategically and successfully used the "lady" emphasis of the day to

[19] Catt and Shuler, *Woman Suffrage and Politics*, p. 14.
[20] Bird, *Born Female*, p. 35.

protest the exploitation of the weak. In so doing, they achieved an upgrading of employment conditions across the board and moved society one giant step in the direction of excellence.

By the dawn of the twentieth century, noticeable change was occurring in the family: "The plain fact is that our present social system is no longer based on the patriarchal family. . . . It is a system in which the wage-earning women form a cardinal factor, a factor which neither reaction nor revolution can eliminate." [21] With World War I and the performance records of women who filled the working gaps left by men, new models became available for what women could do. The decade of the twenties brought a considerable number of women into the professions. But with the Great Depression, both women and Blacks found themselves the last to be hired and the first to be fired.[22]

Women again filled the labor void during World War II, but afterward fled to the home. Though women were elected to membership in the National Academy of Arts and Sciences and won Pulitzer and Nobel Prizes, the focus was upon the home and family. This emphasis remained until the early sixties. In 1962 Eleanor Roosevelt stated: "Because I anticipate success in achieving full employment and full use of America's magnificent potential, I feel confident that in the years ahead many of the remaining outmoded barriers to women's aspirations

[21] Gilbert Murray, "The Weaker Sex," *Educational Review*, XL (1910), 110.
[22] *American Women*, p. 64.

will disappear." [23] Stirrings began to be heard. They were similar to those of Charlotte Stetson at the turn of the century, who mockingly asked in her poem "Homes":

For doth she not bring up her young therein?
And is not rearing young the end of life? [24]

For the neo-feminists these stirrings were the clanking of chains, and they rose up in varying degrees of protest—picketing against sex classification in employment ads, pushing for legalized abortion, marching against marriage bureaus, learning karate, and protesting Miss America and *Playboy*. These scenes were viewed as comedy, or perhaps tragedy —but they got attention and aroused sensitivity to inequities.

During the sixties, women broadened their opportunities to govern at all levels. Angie Brooks of Liberia was elected president of the United Nations General Assembly. Golda Meir became Israel's premier, and Indira Gandhi continued as India's prime minister. Bernadette Devlin became the youngest woman to sit in Britain's House of Commons, and Shirley Chisholm was the first black woman to be elected to Congress. Other sex barriers were broken also: a woman was granted a jockey's license; six women were given permission to work in the Antarctic; and Yale and Princeton were invaded by women. (To be fair I suppose it must be admitted

[23] *Ibid.*
[24] *In This Our World* (Boston: Small, Maynard, & Company, 1899), pp. 7-8.

that the F.B.I.'s Ten Most Wanted list also fell as a masculine domain.) The sixties ended with neo-feminist articles in the major magazines. And the seventies began with a cry for a woman President.[25]

Our struggle to be recognized as equal persons has continued over the years. We have paused in our struggle for "The Negro's Hour" during the Civil War and again for World War I. Then after a decade of achievement in the 1920's, we paused again—for the Great Depression was no time to compete for employment. At times the struggle has progressed, at times regressed—but it has always meant change. Change that is felt—for it cannot just be viewed from afar. It touches government, school, the business and professional world. And most painful to those who would hide, even the home cannot escape its grasp.

[25] Gloria Steinem, "Why We Need a Woman President in 1976," *Look*, XXXIV (January, 1970), 58.

55

4

MISSION AND MIRAGE

One lovely spring morning I got up before the alarm went off. I went to the window to pull back the drapes. The sunbeams danced into the room pantomiming:

This is the day which the Lord has made;
Let us rejoice and be glad in it (Psalm 118:24).

I thought about where we had been as women and where we are today and what we could do about tomorrow. I stood there and looked out at the world and tried to focus on the reality it presents. But I couldn't bring it into clear view. Today's reality seems psychedelic—it swirls and flickers and changes color. It won't hold still. On top of that, each of us glimpses reality from a different perspective, depending upon our individual experiences.

Let's use a pacifier to illustrate this. To the baby, a pacifier is a symbol of security. It means contentment. All is well. His world is complete. To his mother, it is a symbol of solace. Baby is quiet! He has been changed, fed, changed again, rocked, and now he is in his crib with his pacifier and she has a few moments to herself. But ask Grandmother what a pacifier is, and chances are it is a symbol of shame. Now, according to Webster, it is "a usually nipple-shaped device for babies to suck or bite upon." No mention of a symbol of security or solace or shame. Just a cold factual definition with all feeling removed.

But our feelings *are* involved in the living of life; they influence our perception of reality. We just cannot assume that the reality we see is that seen by everyone. Reality is dynamic. We perceive it differently, and we distort it in various ways. These differences in our interpretations are an expression of our uniqueness.

There is a need for us to be open to the reality others express. To be open is not to adopt their reality for our own—though we may do this—but to listen to what they say and accept them as persons of worth, understanding them better as we get clues to the way they view the world.

Usually ideas of reality somewhat merge with each other, but sometimes individual experiences are so different that the views of the observers don't even touch. Two people focus on the same thing, and experience two completely different feelings. This is what causes polarization, one of today's major problems. We see this between fundamentalists and liberals, advocates of Black Power and white supremacists, between the young and the old, the haves and the have-nots. These groups walk along, as did Jack and Ralph in *Lord of the Flies:* "Two continents of experience and feeling, unable to communicate." [1] Wide and dangerous gaps exist.

One of our contributions as women can be to bridge these gaps, to become agents of reconciliation in an age of alienation. This does not mean Lady Bountiful's annual Christmas ritual of filling a basket from her storehouse and knocking on the doors of the poor! Reconciliation calls for interest, willingness, time, study, decision, effort, evaluation, and commitment to a specific problem in a specific place.

One gap is that which exists between the fundamentalists and the liberals. They see the reality of God from different perspectives, and each scoffs at the other's perception and condemns his response to it. The fundamentalists major in the minors by stuffing God in a box on the altar in the sanctuary and shouting "Heresy!" at those who perceive him in the world. And the liberals claim that the fundamentalists won't do anything—just because they don't do what the liberals want them to. Each group denounces the other, and no one listens. The din within the church blocks out the world's cry: "Burn, baby, burn!" We spend our energy putting out brush fires within the church, while blazes from riots and bombings go untended. For the church—when it could be providing a training ground for the bucket brigade and sending its members to put out fires in the world in the spirit of Christ—is often paralyzed by polarization. Women have long been instrumental in directing the church's action both

[1] William Golding, *Lord of the Flies* (New York: G. P. Putnam's Sons, 1959), p. 49.

within its walls and beyond. Perhaps now each of us is being called, within the church, to be a little bridge spanning the abyss between the fundamentalist and the liberal, and, beyond the church, to join the bucket brigade in the world. But whatever else we do as women of faith, we must learn to respect another's perception of God as valid for him. God gave us two ears and only one mouth—surely there's a lesson there!

By now the problem of black and white is an old one, but it continues. Race relations was the topic of discussion at a woman's circle meeting one fall morning. The leader told us that as a child she had lived in "Sundown Town" (where all the Blacks had to be outside the city limits by sundown). She had grown up with the idea that she was not prejudiced, but she certainly wouldn't want her daughter to marry a Negro. She said, "I realize now that in drawing the line at marriage, I was a racist. Because if we truly see *all* persons as created by God, it just doesn't make any difference what color they are." We all agreed, feeling smugly pious about no longer being racists. Having completed our morning as armchair activists, we went home.

A week later there was a racial fight at a newly integrated high school. One of the black students stabbed a white boy. Incidents like this might be circumvented by preventive efforts. We have accumulated enough experience in this area to foresee the problems that may arise: a few white students echo the jeers of their reactionary parents, and a few black students, primed for agitation, react violently. Within the church or the P.T.A., or as neighborhood mothers, women can engage in a preventive plan of educating the two groups of students. The white students involved need to realize that they are blindly accepting their parents' values on this issue, and that neither they nor their parents have sufficient experiential basis for their views. The black students need to realize that, though some of the students will probably try to goad them, these will not be representative, and to respond violently is to play into their hands. Before a situation gets out of hand, perhaps a counseling psychologist could be sponsored to lead a small mixed guidance group composed of the students most likely headed for trouble. One of our contributions as women can be preventive efforts; certainly our habitual armchair activism is not enough.

There is much talk today of the generation gap. Our place in the world looked different to us from the eyes of life's springtime than it does today in our summertime. For many of our dreams have remained fantasies. We know the feelings of *The Embezzler*, Guy Prime, who in his youth had aspired "to be everything in the world, regardless of incompatibilities: to be a poet and a millionaire, a Don Juan and a family man, a gallant soldier on the battlefield and a general at headquarters clinking with medals." But later in life "the attainable universe seemed suddenly to have shrunk to what? To the brokerage house and the country club!" [2] What

[2] Louis Auchincloss, *The Embezzler* (Boston: Houghton Mifflin Company, 1966), p. 193.

we see now differs from the perspective of emerging youth. We want to tell them that their dreams cannot be fulfilled—but they won't hear. We want to share with them our wisdom—they aren't interested. They look at the world we have created and condemn us.

Dr. Cynthia Clark Wedel, a psychologist and first woman president of the National Council of Churches, suggests:

Having been closest to their children in the youngsters' formative years, women often may be in the best position to extend the sympathy and understanding needed to bridge the generation gap. But to do this, they must listen intently to their children's ideas and views without instantly judging them on the standards by which they were judged a generation ago.[3]

We accomplish nothing by shouting at each other. We must listen and take one another seriously. Beyond the home, panel discussions, made up of representatives from both ends of the generation gap, have been tried with some success. These, when the participants are unrelated, have been helpful in bringing about better understanding of the problems that each sees. Perhaps one of our contributions as women, through the church or other groups, can be the sponsoring of these discussions in our own communities. For through listening—being sensitive to the other's view of reality—we gain understanding and insight into this age-old problem that seems intensified at this point in our history.

[3] "Challenge to American Women: Building a New Morality for Our Youth," *Family Weekly* (March 29, 1970).

There is a gap between the "good" man and the "bad" man. Surely reality regarding right and wrong is stable and clear-cut—but so often, not so. We get involved in situational ethics. My daughter Valerie is already aware of this. One morning when she was four, I was washing her hair, and she was telling me about her dream the night before:

"Mommy, I dreamed about a bad man last night."

"You did?"

"Well, no. I mean he wasn't a bad man. He was a good man. He just did some bad things."

I have always filed those who are responsible for crime and violence in the "bad" category. It has been a stable category all these years—until I read Mario Puzo's *The Godfather*, which is a novel about one of the heads of La Cosa Nostra. Puzo pointed out in a way that reached me for the first time that, if we go back far enough, those who are responsible for crime and violence are sometimes the "good" men—men who do not commit crime or participate in violence, but who demean the humanness of the disadvantaged. The unfortunates look into the future and see only a vicious cycle of birth and poverty and death, birth and poverty and death. They escape through crime. They react to the inhumanity of those who, *without even noticing*, would press them under. Michael, the Godfather's son, understands this: "My father . . . doesn't accept the rules of the society we live in because those rules would have condemned him to a life not suitable to a man like himself, a man of extraordinary force and character. . . . He refuses to live by rules . . . which condemn

him to a defeated life." [4] After reading *The Godfather,* I certainly don't condone crime—but I can
no longer automatically write off the criminal. We
must listen. We must understand his reality. This is
a world totally alien to most of us, but we cannot
be effective reconcilers if we remain ignorant.

Perhaps as women we can be of most help to
juvenile offenders. We can talk with the local juvenile authorities to see where we can best be of
service. We may be needed as volunteer tutors within the public school system. Chuck, a junior high
school student, was academically capable, but he
needed special help in reading. He could top his
classmates in math, but fumbled so in reading that
he was laughed at and ridiculed. One day he'd had
enough, and this large quiet boy turned around and
socked his chief antagonist; he knocked out two
teeth and broke the boy's jaw. He was not a delinquent. He needed a reading tutor.

Some students simply need someone to give them
special attention, to take the time to show them
that they are important individuals. Take a girl
named Virginia, who was withdrawn and apathetic,
and didn't care about her appearance. She ducked
her head when she talked with adults. She did not
relate to other students, and they did not even notice
her. She began to stay home from school more and
more frequently—and was finally charged with tru-
ancy. Our giving a few hours a week could mean
hope for the Virginias and the Chucks.

It will take much more than a few hours to meet

[4] (New York: G. P. Putnam's Sons, 1969), p. 363.

the foster child's need. Joan had spent ten of her thirteen years being shifted from one foster home to another. Some foster parents had barely fed her and used the balance of her meager support allowance for themselves. In these homes she was usually just one of several foster children. In others she was Cinderella—without a good fairy. She hadn't yet stumbled on to a mature and responsible family that would be a good model for her own adult years. One of the great needs for children in our society is responsible adults, willing to share their homes and themselves with a foster child.

To become better informed, we can observe the juvenile courts to learn how youth are treated and how they respond. We can visit the detention centers for minors to experience this part of their world. We can push for these to become places of rehabilitation, which teach the students how to be responsible persons in society—instead of how to be good inmates. Perhaps with a better perspective of the world of juvenile offenders, we can learn how to communicate with them and begin to help them build a life free from violence.

The social issues of our time are complex, and their intensity is increased by polarization. There is a dire need for attempts at reconciliation—for hearing and sharing and understanding and mutual respect. But how difficult it is for us to affirm the worth of one whose opinions and actions are contrary to our own convictions, to accept his stance as valid for him, to acknowledge that some of his points are well taken, to activate cooperative efforts to create a better society. How difficult it is to actualize reconciliation! It is so much easier for us to ignore the problems or offer pat solutions or pretend we aren't responsible.

How I envy the woman who can pretend that all is well! The one like Alix Prime in *The Embezzler,* who was "so insulated from horror, that she picked her way across the carnage of the universe without daring to look down."[5] She simply pretends the problems do not exist. She sweeps them under the rug and refuses to perceive them. What a beautiful mirage! Except that it blinds us to our mission.

All of us do this to some extent. The sufferings in the world have become like Novocain. We become numb to the pain. One of my friends recently returned from India and told me about the men, rather like our garbage collectors, who, each morning, gather the dead bodies from the streets and dump them into a large hole. I can use these words, but I keep their meaning away from me, out there at a safe distance—in India—so that I will not have to feel its horror. We choose *not* to perceive. We choose to insulate ourselves.

I also envy the bigot. She is not confused. She lifts up her reality as the only possibility. She *knows* she is right. She does not need to be open to another's view—for she has all the answers. She can be rigid and inflexible. Everything is so simple: Black is black, and white is white/Wrong is wrong, and right is right. What a glorious mirage! Except that it blinds us to our mission.

Like the bigot, we tend to sigh in relief when we

[5] Auchincloss, *The Embezzler,* p. 162.

make a decision: "There, that's over." And we close ourselves to any possibility of changing—let alone reversing—our decisions and actions. We need to be continually sensitive to the reality that others see, not only to understand them better, but also to broaden and permit our own views of reality to grow.

I am most envious of the woman who believes that she is God's puppet. She just puts herself in God's hands, and she doesn't have to concern herself with the world. All she has to do is get right with God—and let her neighbor do the same. What a comfortable mirage! Except that it blinds us to our mission.

In these troubled times all of us are looking for stability. We are searching for simplicity in our complex society. If only we were puppets whose strings God pulls, instead of free persons responsible for our own decisions and the world we shape. If only we could *know* what is right—what is God's will. Father Yánaros, in *The Fratricides*, shares our dilemma as he prays to God:

What joy it would be and what relief if You commanded, if You simply ordered: do this; don't do that! If I only knew what You want! Oh, to be able to live, to act, to desire, with certainty! Now, all is chaos, and I, the worm, must bring order! [*]

We must bring order! And we must bring it in the midst of insoluble problems. Carl Jung once remarked that the serious problems of life are never solved, and if it seems they are, something impor-

[*] Kazantzakis, *The Fratricides*, p. 177.

tant has been lost.[7] Perhaps we must learn to live with the tensions of insoluble problems—ever listening, ever confronting, ever grappling, ever searching —but never finishing, never solving. And yet the search keeps us from being complete victims of the problems, for we create a new way to view them. The problems remain. But care is born. Hope is born. For we live in this tension together. When we listen and confront and try to understand, we do so within human relationships. We share together the knowledge of the problems. We struggle together to create a better way. And the struggle itself is significant. It is meaningful. We find hope in that the struggle does not die, but continues. And because we find hope, we continue to struggle to bring order in the midst of insoluble problems.

We must bring order! And we must bring it without the certainty that we are right. How can we judge? What is our standard to measure the rightness and wrongness of our decisions? Robert Crichton gives us an example of this difficulty in *The Secret of Santa Vittoria*:

"I did some bad things," von Prum said. "See? I know that. But everything I did was for the country."

"What you forget," Caterina told him, "is that every place is someone's country." [8]

Perhaps we need to shift our focal point from the issues to the persons involved—the ones who create the problems and the ones who are victimized. As Christians we take the life of Christ as our model.

[7] Cited in Rollo May, *Love and Will*, reprint from *Psychology Today*, III (August, 1969), 61.

[8] (New York: Simon and Schuster, 1966), p. 401.

If an act is harmful to one in need, it is wrong. But this is not enough. For if our *in*action is harmful to another in need, it too is wrong. For Christ not only made decisions, he also acted upon them.

When we lived in Massachusetts, we had some friends whose land went back in their family to the Queen's Grant. Over a mantle in their old historic home hangs a musket called Old Betsy. One evening Tom told us about Old Betsy. It had belonged to his great-great-great-great-grandfather, Ebenezer, who was a young man at the time of the Revolutionary War. He had a vision. He used to sit on the front porch with Old Betsy in his lap, rocking and thinking about how George Washington would appear over the hill riding a beautiful white stallion, and call: "Ebenezer Whittaker, we need *you!*"

One day as he sat rocking and envisioning Washington coming for him, here came reality in the form of Obadiah Morris, running up from the next farm over. His clothes were dirty and torn, and he hollered out, "Hey, Eb! Quick! Grab your gun and let's get. All hell's broke loose at Concord!"

But, no! No! Ebenezer didn't go. He sat there and rocked—waiting. He waited for his dream to come true. Waited for George Washington to ride over the hill—and Old Betsy has never been fired.

God has formed us, and here we are—confronted with the problems of a fragmented world. We are free to rock it out, enclosing ourselves within a mirage. Or we can accept our mission, living our lives for others in need, involving ourselves in forming a new world in the spirit of Christ. As women of faith in action, *we* must try to bring order.

5

WITH UNIQUENESS AND WORTH

We must bring order. We've known for a long time that "it's God's will" was just an excuse for our own irresponsibility. But we haven't wanted to admit this to ourselves—let alone to anyone else. We've known because there is no way to reconcile the social conditions of our world with the will of a loving God. But our puppet habit is old and hard to break, and since God wouldn't play our game, the image-makers came along and provided us with strings.

We "strut and fret our hour upon the stage" as always. (Unless we're militant feminists who refuse to strut, and simply fret over woman's being number two!) The drama unfolds according to the script of the ad men and the image-makers. We buy the things and join the clubs that we are told give us reason to strut. And then we corporately fret over the bills and the ulcers and our lack of time. (And individually, secretly, over our insatiable emptiness —but let us not think of that; let us concentrate on image.) There's a string for every occasion. The script tells us what to say and do, and even what to believe. We become like Eddie, in *The Arrangement*, when he talks to himself:

"Sir, why do they call you a Nothing?"
"Because that's what I am."
"What do you do in life?"
"Nothing."
"Are you a businessman?"
"No."
"Then what are you?"
"Nothing."
"What do you love, sir?"
"Nothing."
"Not even yourself?"
"Especially not that!"
"What do you hate then?"
"Nothing." . . .
"Are you a believer?"
"No."
"An unbeliever?"
"Of course not. I'm a Nothing."
"Why do you keep smiling all the time?"
"Do I?"
"Yes, you keep smiling at me; at least I think that's a smile. What is that? Where your face should be?"
"Nothing." [1]

We are for what we are supposed to be for and against what we are supposed to be against. But, in actuality, we care very little and really stand for nothing. We are just blobs with empty smiles. We imprison ourselves within the glass walls of image and peek at the world without touching it or being touched by it. To keep others from knowing we are not who we pretend to be, we avoid the risk of close

[1] Elia Kazan, *The Arrangement* (New York: Stein & Day, 1967), p. 116.

relationships and lose the ability to be sensitive to the feelings and needs of others. We move about within our fragile mass-produced image—and fail to discover the beauty and excellence of the individual self.

In a small group of young mothers, one woman cried out in desperation: "I'm just not that good, sweet, kind, ever-patient madonna I'm supposed to be! How long can I pretend I am?" And the word to her was hurled into the cosmos: You don't have to pretend. You're an individual created by God. You're unique, unrepeatable, irreplaceable, and un-exchangeable. Because God created you, you *are* a person of worth.

We are persons of worth! When we were given life, we were given worth. Isn't it astounding! All those things we do that we shouldn't—and all those things we don't do that we should! And by God's grace we are still persons of worth! Sometimes I can't see my worth for my guilt, and I don't like myself. In these moments I feel frustrated and inadequate and that I'm misusing my gift of life. I think this is what Frankl is talking about when he speaks of the tension "between what one has already achieved and what one still ought to accomplish, or the gap between what one is and what one should become." [2]

One of my friends who is a minister was adopted when he was a small boy by parents whom he could never quite please. No matter how well he did, they always wanted him to do a little better. Once he

[2] *Man's Search for Meaning,* pp. 105-6.

overheard them tell their friends, "Well, you know, you can't expect very much of an *adopted* child." The way they sneered "adopted" sent chills of loneliness down his spine. In junior high he almost went off the deep end—until he heard the word that he was a child of God. He was God's child! A person of worth. When he acknowledged this relationship with God, he felt he could stand up straight and accept life on whatever terms it offered.

I know a woman who talks of her relationship with God in terms of: "I ask God if it's his will every time before I even go to the beauty shop," or, "If I'm in a hurry, I just ask God to find me a parking place." OK, this is reality for her. But not for me. My relationship with God just *is*. I am his creature. I see him as Father. All that I *am* is his gift. All that I *do* is my response to him.

When my life is rippling along like a gentle stream, or at night when I check our four lovely sleeping children, I bubble over with joy. I cry out silently from the core of my being, "Oh, Father. Glory be to Thee." And when I come to life's waterfalls and go thundering down into the depths of despair and feel life's pain, I cry out in desperation, "Oh, Father." But in that moment, I must also say, "Glory be to Thee." For I still *am*. I have *life*.

My relationship with God is not my bit in church or my monologue in prayer—it is *all* my life. This is it. Here I am. My relationship with God is the power that gives me worth and assures me I can reach toward my potentialities on whatever terms life offers. At the same time this relationship is the prodder that pushes me into the world to try to make it a better place for all people. Sartre says that a man defines himself by his acts. My monologue with God is hollow unless it is accompanied by my deeds. I can do little, but I must at least do that. We have been given life, and our relationship with God calls us to be who we are, with the courage to stand. Alone when necessary. With the minority when necessary. But to stand and act, and thus define ourselves as ones who are in relationship with God.

For not to stand, not to act, is to respond that it doesn't matter. We are created by God. It doesn't matter. God *gave* us life. It doesn't matter. We are *alive* this moment. It doesn't matter. Nietzsche joins this chorus: "In the long run, one life means nothing." This is a tragic attitude, for it means spiritual death. It beats down our ability to imagine and therefore create a better life for ourselves and our brothers. It snuffs out our desire to give ourselves in love. It stifles our capacity for commitment. All of us have had this attitude at times. We have wept with Gennaro in A *Last Lamp Burning:* "for the lost, the impossible, dream of personal freedom, of individual dignity and of a rightful place in the world. Wept for all the weary, uncomprehending struggle that was life day-by-day, year-by-year." [3] It doesn't matter. We are born, and we cry. We die, and we are put in a box. And in between . . . .

And in between is *life*. It *matters*. In *The Secret of Santa Vittoria,* Babbaluche says:

[3] Gwyn Griffin, A *Last Lamp Burning* (New York: G. P. Putnam's Sons, 1966), p. 397.

73

Think. This is the end of it. All of those years of work and pain and sickness, all the hopes I had as a young man, and this—this—is the end. Nothing more. Can you imagine it? That I came all those miles and all those years for this? That my mother starved those years to bring me to this? Isn't that strange? [4]

It is enough. It matters. For all those years, he lived his life. Life itself is significant. His friend Bombolini affirms this, for he says: "In the end, nothing is more important than one life." [5] It matters.

Our significance is not something we earn. It is a gift from God. We just *are* significant. As long as I can remember I've wanted to be an author—for that, I told myself, would make me significant. I could just picture myself in a fashionable suit, not a hair out of place. I'd stand beside a large mahogany desk and behind me—floor to ceiling and wall to wall—would be rows and rows of books. In my fantasy I watched myself extend my hand to my publisher as he said, "Congratulations! You're an author!" Ah-h-h—significance!

One morning a few years ago, Bill came bounding into the children's room with a letter in his hand. I was hopping over toys making a bed, still in my nightie, with my hair flopping down in my face.

"Marilyn! Guess what! You're an author!"

But—no! No! I'm still just me!

Just me—and yet, significance was mine from the beginning. We are all significant—not because of what we have done or who we are, but simply because we were born. Tillich tells us: "The world

[4] Crichton, *The Secret of Santa Vittoria*, p. 386.
[5] *Ibid.*, p. 368.

would not be what it is without *this* individual self." [6] To realize that life, life itself, is significant calls us from the spiritual death of nihilism. To realize that significance is innate calls us to spiritual life. We are capable of living in the present and reaching beyond it into the future.

But as we reach into the future, we tremble with all our ancestors throughout the ages of man. For we share the feelings of the caveman in Michener's *The Source:* "And the anguish that Ur knew that night—the mystery of death, the triumph of evil, the terrible loneliness of being alone, the discovery that self of itself is insufficient—is the anxiety that torments the world to this day." [7] Is each of us significant? Yes! Self-sufficient? No!

Jesus said, "For where two or three are gathered in my name, there am I in the midst of them" (Matthew 18:20). The Word exists in community. Our spiritual life may be seen as *inner life,* but its growth is dependent upon our *inter-life.* When allowed to exist, our creative spirit looks into the future and provides a vision of what might be for ourselves and our brothers. It calls us to love, and then we stretch toward commitment.

The last scene in the movie *Midnight Cowboy* provides us with an illustration of relationship as well as of significance. Ricco has always in reality stumbled into a future of despair, but always in fantasy strolled in the sand of a Florida beach. Now he is dying, but he and his friend Joe Buck are on their way to Florida. They are two human beings

[6] *The Courage to Be,* p. 88.
[7] (New York: Random House, 1965), p. 96.

who have known suffering and shame and loneliness and violence—but also hope. They ride along; time passes. Ricco sleeps. In caring for Ricco, Joe is challenged to create a better way of living. He says to his friend that he's decided to get a job. But his friend no longer sleeps; he has died. The other passengers turn around and stare, curious and fearful, and Joe puts his arm around his dead friend.

As they ride on together, we see death as a part of life; we see the importance of relationships; we feel the impact of loneliness and uncertainty. Ricco succeeded in nothing. But he died his death while fulfilling a dream. He was a person with uniqueness and worth. He was significant. With Joe's arm around him, they ride into the darkness. And in that silent darkness, we know that the world is not what it was—for it no longer includes Ricco's stumbling and dreaming—it is minus Ricco's individual self.

Each person is unique. Each person is significant as part of the whole. This much is given. Requiring of ourselves the best use of our capabilities for the benefit of all mankind is not a prerequisite to worth, but a response to the wonder of it!

6

MONOLOGUES EN MASSE

One afternoon last summer I left cars and houses and people behind and rode to the top of a ridge of Black Mountain near Creede, Colorado. The steady rocking climb of the horse gave rhythm to the gentle rustling of the forest. Above me in the distance Old Bristol Head reached into the sky, rugged and strong. Far to the west, peaked with snow, the Rio Grande Pyramid rose against the horizon, stately and majestic. I looked down from the top of the ridge far below to three rippling lakes linked together by a winding blue ribbon, the shrunken size of the river reflecting the depth of the green valley. A lane of brown thread cut into the green and led to a single log cabin, the only sign of human existence. As I stood alone on the ridge, surrounded by the magnificence of the unmarred wilderness, I breathed into my being the luxury of solitude. I gazed in awe at this enchanted view of earth as a manless expanse, still and timeless, uncrowded and unchanging.

But abruptly and harshly the magic moment ended as my mind's eye recalled the view of earth as seen from the moon. For this manless expanse was transformed into a tiny planet orbiting the sun.

It became an Apollo teeming with three billion astronauts, spinning in a noisy hubbub, in a chorus of mass monologues.

May describes our situation:

> We must protect ourselves from . . . the barrage of words and noise from radio and TV, from the cacophonous din and the hordes of anonymous humanity in the rush-hour subway, from the assembly-line of collectivized industry and gigantic factory-modeled multiversities. It is a schizoid world in which numbers inexorably take over as our means of identification, like creeping lava threatening to suffocate and fossilize all breathing life in its path.[1]

Each of us seems to stand alone in the midst of this horde of humanity, to have to protect himself from the masses crowding in upon him. This problem is the product of overpopulation and urbanization, and it is a major psychological obstacle to caring for one another. How can I respond to those I'm trying to protect myself against!

The problem of human relatedness is a vital one in today's world. There is a need for awareness that the masses consist of individual persons, each with uniqueness and worth. There is a need for authenticity, as gamesmanship rules out both spontaneity and intimacy. Perhaps as women this is an area in which we can make an impact.

We have almost lost the art of dialogue. It has become outmoded by the press of humanity and the anonymity of technology. I frequently watch Johnny Carson. He's like an old friend. I'd say "hi" to him if I saw him on the street. But he isn't even

[1] *Love and Will*, p. 23.

aware of me. I have spent hours in his presence—and he doesn't even know I exist. I'm invisible. I'm anonymous. I'm unnecessary. His monologue to the masses goes on with or without me. I don't like to think about that. It's painful. There is no opportunity for dialogue.

The same thing happens in the family. The center of family life is oftentimes TV. We focus on the boob-tube with little awareness of each other—except to say "Be quiet!" or "Move! I can't see!" There is no dialogue. Ionesco's play, *The Bald Soprano*, points up our lack of awareness within the family. A man and woman meet and begin to talk with each other. They learn that they both came to New York on the same train from New Haven. They even have the same Fifth Avenue address. In fact, they live in the same apartment, and both have a seven-year-old daughter. Finally, they discover they are man and wife!

Unawareness reigns in our monological age, but occasionally the attitude of a sensitive person prompts dialogue. One of my husband's relatives has always impressed me as being different from other people, but I didn't realize in what way until last summer. John had spent the night with us, and after Bill went to work, we had a second cup of coffee. My youngest child Bryant was playing with a ball. After a little while, John started playing ball with him and stopped talking to me. He even left my question hanging in midair. A few minutes later he stopped playing ball and began talking with me again. He ignored Bryant's efforts to regain his attention. At that moment I realized what made him different: he really concentrates when he relates to another. He gives his complete attention. No wonder I always feel slightly uneasy in conversations with him. He's listening! He's hearing! He's taking me seriously! I'm just not used to that. Usually when I have coffee with friends, we engage in dual monologues—with each of us enthralled with our own words and ideas.

Most of our relationships are functional and positional rather than personal. We do not invest ourselves. In *The Arrangement*, Eddie realizes this:

Did anyone care? Why should they? Did I? Surprisingly little! I realized I did not have and never had had any friends. My relationships—those I did have—were either professional or functional. . . . But you couldn't call these friendships. I hadn't talked or related to any of these people, except for some use or function. I hadn't touched any of them humanly. They were things to me.[2]

This kind of relatedness is necessary in today's world. But we need also to share authentic relationships with others; we need to invest ourselves and to be invested in.

A couple of my friends, Peggy and Don, at various times have invited boys with problems to live with them. Steve, who is eighteen, lives with them now. One day he became angry and said he wanted to leave. Peggy packed up the children and took Steve to the expressway so he could hitchhike—realizing that he had to be assured of his freedom to leave and at the same time knowing he'd be back. One of her children cried on the way home after leaving

[2] Kazan, *The Arrangement*, p. 480.

him. Steve returned in less than an hour, and a few days later he and Peggy were laughing about it. "You know," Peggy told him, "Sally cried all the way home and asked why I didn't leave instead." Steve stopped laughing and was silent for a moment. Then he looked at her through a cloud of tears. "She really did? No one's ever cried over *me* before."

We need to be cried over. We need to be involved in personal relationships. The research of René Spitz has shown that a baby must receive mothering care if he is to develop; otherwise, he withers away and remains in a stupor. We need to care and to be cared for.

During her experience as a counseling psychologist, Leona Tyler has changed her position regarding her response to others. Writing in 1956, she states: "I used to say to myself . . . , '*He must like me*. Whatever else happens here, by the time the hour is over, he must like me, at least a little.' I don't put it quite that way now. Rather, I say to myself, '*We must like each other*.' " [3] In *The Work of the Counselor* in 1969, she moved to the position: "*I must like him*." From *he* must like *me*, to *we* must like *each other*, to *I* must like *him*. We can profit from her experience in our investment in others.

Let's look at what happens when the goal of relatedness is to be liked. I tell myself that I am concerned about another, but my focus is on *my* concern and how to show it, rather than actually focusing on the *other person*. I am so conscious of

[3] "The Initial Interview," *Personnel and Guidance Journal*, XXXIV (April, 1956), 467.

myself that I cannot really see anyone else. I confuse my own sentiment with care.

Sentiment focuses on ourselves rather than on another. We revel in the emotion—it is self-centered. Care, on the other hand, focuses on the other person and leads to investment through a supporting human relationship. It is other-centered. It is easy to drown ourselves in our own sentiment—and never touch the other person with care.

To move from "he must like me" to "we must like each other" is a step forward. When this is my goal, I become as concerned with liking as I am with being liked. My focal point is not limited to myself; I also see the other person. I become less self-conscious and more aware of others. This awareness may be risky at first. I may not like what I see. I may not be pleased about being in orbit with a particular individual. For a while in her nightly prayers, my daughter Valerie had the habit of saying: "Dear God, thank you for my friends—and my other friends." It is the "other friends" that make this goal difficult.

We are human and imperfect. At times we are thoughtless and insensitive; we misunderstand others and reject them. We are neglectful and resentful. And they are, too. In A Thousand Clowns the social worker says about a little boy: "I didn't like Raymond Ledbetter so I tried to understand him, and now that I understand him, I hate him." Hostility is a part of life; it is a part of every life—some people just hide it a little deeper than others. May says: "Hate and love are not polar opposites; they go

together, particularly in transitional ages like ours." [4]
We love our children and sometimes become extremely angry with them. There are unappealing characteristics in those closest to us. In the same way, there are attributes we will appreciate in persons we don't like—if we bother to discover them.

This brings us to a new goal in relatedness: "I must like him." It isn't so important that we impress others as it is that we care for them. We find ourselves living life with another as we learn what she wants, how she feels about her children, the things she has done that she takes pride in, and the things that worry her. We begin to listen to her and to accept her as she is. We begin to speak to her, affirming her as an individual with uniqueness and worth.

One of the obstacles to self-investment is the mobility rate. It means a continual shuffle of people across the country. How difficult it is to leave those who have become so much a part of our lives. Kazantzakis captures the hurt in moving:

What good are tears? . . . Let's get it over with! But quickly, quickly, before our hearts break, before we fully realize the tragedy. Hurry, friends, lend a hand! It is difficult, you see, very difficult for the soul to tear itself away from familiar soil and familiar waters. [5]

We, too, move quickly. We are jerked one day from a farewell party in one group and thrust the next into a welcome reception in another locale! We smile both times—but we are sad. A little boy

[4] *Love and Will*, p. 42.
[5] *The Fratricides*, p. 12.

and his mother were visiting a friend with a six-week-old baby girl. The little boy begged and begged to take the baby home. The friend explained that they just couldn't get along without her. He looked puzzled and asked: "Well, if you used to get along without her before you got her, why can't you get along without her now?" Moving is like that. We can get along without our friends if we have to, but the experience is painful. We suffer until we begin to know and care for the individuals in our new community. They don't really replace our old friends —for they will always be part of us. But the dynamic of love becomes active in our lives again as we give ourselves to these new persons.

Another reason we fail to give ourselves away is the fear that we will have nothing left. This fear is justified if people are taking from us—if we are neurotically being drained by the neurotics in our community. But to be taken from is not a gift. To be taken from is to allow ourselves to be a victim of someone's demands. We feel our time is stolen from us. We become resentful. But to freely decide to fulfill someone's need is a gift—a gift that replenishes itself. In *Daughter of Silence*, Peter and Ninette are talking:

"There are times," [said Peter] "when I wonder if I am not destroying in myself what I'm trying to build in others. . . . How do you renew in yourself what you spend on others?"

"If I could be sure of the answer to that," said Ninette softly, "I would feel safer than I do now. But I think—no, I believe—that the spending is the growing too, that the flowers fall to make the fruit grow, and that this is the way it was intended to be from the beginning." [6]

It is in giving ourselves away that we find ourselves.

It would be good to be able to point to the local church as an example of a corporate body with the courage to give itself away. However, this is seldom the case. How often laymen and ministers avoid involvement with the excuse: "We really feel we must wait until we have a wholeness within the congregation before we can go out into the community to be in mission." These laymen and these ministers will always wait. They will mark time in place while God's world moves on. For a community of faith, being made up of people, also finds itself by giving itself away. If it is to be faithful, it will not seek love within its walls but will share love through service to God's people who suffer in the world.

We can actually call others into being by investing ourselves in them. Reuel Howe says:

Love calls forth persons and reunites life with life by providing the relationships in which the created needs of men are met. The environment of saving love is needed to produce out of our biological nature and the physical world in which we live the image of God in each of us and the Kingdom of God for all of us. [7]

Everyone wants to be loved. This is natural. But if the world is to move toward the Kingdom of God,

[6] West, *Daughter of Silence*, p. 52.

[7] *Herein Is Love* (Valley Forge, Pa.: Judson Press, 1961), p. 81.

some of us must shift our emphasis. We must concentrate on how to love others—rather than on how to get them to love us. One of our tasks as Christians is to strive—not to be loved—but to love. Erich Fromm tells us: "While one is consciously afraid of not being loved, the real though usually unconscious fear is that of loving." [8]

As Christians, we take the life of Christ as our model. We have been shown what it means to live life loving rather than seeking love. We have been shown a love that gives freely without demand and fully without reservation. If our love is to encompass more than those for whom we easily feel rapport— if we are to embrace those who are not of kindred spirit—we must work at it. Where love is not our response, it becomes our responsibility. It must be practiced. Fromm states:

With regard to the art of loving, . . . anyone who aspires to become a master in this art must begin by practicing discipline, concentration and patience throughout every phase of his life. . . . To be concentrated in relation to others means primarily to be able to listen. [9]

Our concentration is not on playing the proper game—but on listening. This, of course, does not mean listening to our own monologue or the buzz of the masses. It means being sensitive to another.

Eric Berne concludes his book, *Games People Play*, in the following way:

[8] *The Art of Loving* (New York: Bantam Books, 1963), p. 107.
[9] *Ibid.*, p. 93.

For certain fortunate people there is something which transcends all classifications of behavior, and that is awareness; something which rises above the programing of the past, and that is spontaneity; and something that is more rewarding than games, and that is intimacy. . . . This may mean that there is no hope for the human race, but there is hope for individual members of it.[10]

Awareness, spontaneity, and intimacy—it is through dialogue that we have an opportunity to develop these qualities, to share them, and to call them forth in others. The woman of faith speaks with authenticity, listens with sensitivity, and responds with love. *availability + discernment*

[10] (New York: Grove Press, 1964), p. 184.

7

ONE FOR ANOTHER

The faithful pre–twenty-first century woman is like the caveman Ur in *The Source*, who was "a man who had been a happy, indistinct member of a group living in a cave, and now he was asked to be Ur, one man standing by himself." [1] We are happy indistinct members of a group living in a cave. What a comfortable place to be! It shelters us from the world beyond. It protects us from discomforting associations with those who suffer from deprivation. We have food and clothes and warmth in the winter time. How blissful life is from inside the cave. We are satisfied with our world the way it is. Jess expresses this in *Except for Me and Thee*:

The world suits me to a T, Mattie. That's my trouble. Why, sometimes I think the Lord made it especially for me. I like its colors. I don't see how the flavor of spring water could be improved on. I'd hate to have to try to invent a better fruit than a Grimes Golden. Yellow lamplight on white snow. Thee ever seen anything prettier? Out here alone, this quirk of mine seems a blessing. I feel downright joyful. [2]

[1] Michener, *The Source*, p. 85.
[2] West, *Except for Me and Thee*, p. 283.

I have known this joy, too. There are moments when it wells up inside of me, and I know total bliss and peace and happiness: The last few winters when I would rock our babies in front of the fireplace, enjoying the flickering and crackling of the warm fire. And when the smell of hot cinnamon rolls floats through the house. And when Bill is home in the evening and I glance across the room at him comfortably engrossed in a book. These are cherished moments.

I would like to just sit out the pre–twenty-first century in my cave with other passive members of my group. But I get busy fixing dinner and forget to turn off TV after "Sesame Street," and the news comes on. And for the moment, the outside world enters my cave, and I am stung by the cruelties and injustices. While I rock my babies in front of a glowing fire, sickly babes are shivering in unheated tenements. While my children enjoy a snack of hot cinnamon rolls, the stomachs of Biafran children bloat from starvation. While Bill and I build our library, there are people around the globe who cannot even read and write.

I sigh in distress and shake my head and wring my hands in worry. And then I shut my eyes, along with others living in the cave, and we pray for those poor people outside. We are like Updike's Piet, who said to his partner: "Matt, frankly, I don't think I'm calling any of the shots any more. All I can do is let things happen, and pray." And Matt's response cuts into our consciences: "That's all you ever do." [3] Prayer is important, but it is not enough.

[3] *Couples*, p. 412.

Prayer that is passive does not warm the tenements or feed the hungry or teach the illiterate. If our prayers are to be more than empty words of sentiment, we must open our eyes and become the instruments of their fulfillment.

We would prefer the security accessible in just putting ourselves in God's hands. That would be so much easier than having to *be* his hands. Would that we were God's puppets! That we could simply fold up in passivity, and he would pull the right strings at the right time! Ah! To be Melba Milquetoast bending with the wind: "I'm yours, Lord. Do what you will with me. I'll wait for you to move me." But the trouble is, the planet spins on and Melba doesn't move. She has no strings—no strings attached. She is free. And therefore responsible.

No, Piet's response will not do. Christ is our model, and he acted out his prayers. He loved those within the cave, but he lived in the world beyond it. Father Yánaros told the cloistered monks: "Today prayer means deeds. . . . The real Christ walks with the people, struggles with them, is crucified with them, is resurrected with them." [4] We are called from the blind comfort and pretension of the cave. Like Ur, each of us who would follow Christ is asked to be one individual, willing to risk standing alone for the sake of another.

To step outside the cave is to see face-to-face these strangers who share with us the commonality of creation. Kazantzakis sketches a "small child, withered from hunger, with a swollen green belly,"

[4] Kazantzakis, *The Fratricides*, p. 20.

lying in the middle of the road, "digging the earth and eating the soil." The priest's eyes fill with tears.

"Get up, my child. Are you hungry?"

"No I just finished eating."

"What did you eat?"

The child stretches out his hand and shows him. "Dirt."

The priest groans.

The world is rotten, he thought, rotten and unjust. My God, how can You hold it in Your arms without hurling it down and smashing it into a thousand pieces? So . . . You can shape a new world—a better one! Don't You see that this child is hungry? Can't You see it's eating dirt?

Then he bows his head in shame. "No, my Lord, it's not Your fault. I'm to blame, we are all guilty for this child who eats dirt." [5]

Each of us is slapped with the question, "What do I?" For we—being free to work toward a better way—are responsible for this little child who eats dirt. He is a symbol of all the "least of these" who are hungry and thirsty, naked and sick.

The woman of faith decides to live her life on their behalf. No one requires this of her. Her life is her own, and she can waste it or horde it or sell it or give it away. She is free to live her life for herself. She is free to say, "What's mine's mine, and I'm going to keep it." She is even free to say, "What's yours is mine, and I'm going to take it." But she *decides* to say, "What's mine is yours, and I'm

[5]*Ibid.*, pp. 47-48.

going to share it." She decides to follow the way of Christ—to live her life for others.

Our society is geared toward extrinsic rewards. We put grades on schoolpapers, give prizes for paintings, compete for medals and trophies. The church has given attendance pins, promised the "good feeling" after worship, and dangled heaven as a bribe toward do-goodism. It is difficult for us to think in terms of mercy rather than justice. If we are equally worthy, equally significant, no matter how responsible or irresponsible we are, why sacrifice? Why bother? It isn't just! It isn't fair! But when we have shared ourselves in order to gain something, we have not *given* ourselves away; we have *sold* ourselves!

The woman of faith does not share herself for a reward, but simply in response. She cannot work her way into God's grace; she is already there. She cannot earn acceptance; she already has it. She is part of the family—whether she likes it or not—whether we like it or not. She responds with the knowledge that her reward is not extrinsic. Her giving of herself *is* her reward.

One summer some visitors were looking at the toys in a child development center in a poverty area. One of the toys was a little wooden door hinged to a plywood cube. There were several kinds of hooks and locks that had to be undone to get the door open. One of the women went through the whole process, opened the door eagerly, and then, disappointed, asked: "What's supposed to be inside?" Where's my reward? The opening of the door itself—the doing of the deed—was her reward. And so it is with us.

The faithful pre–twenty-first century woman stands as a committed person in an age of apathy. In the midst of her comfort and leisure, she lives a sacrificial life. There is no reward involved. She remains a part of the family whether or not she does this. Being aware of her worth as a person and the significance of her life, she decides to respond by giving herself away.

8

ADVENTURE IN ACTION

The unique traits that women develop in caring for the nuclear family can meet specific needs on a community level. Nevitt Sanford suggests:

Our greatest tasks at the present time have to do with the development and improvement of people, with the expansion and enrichment of their lives, with the improvement of their relations one to another, and with the development and maintenance of communities in which these things are possible.[1]

This is an area that men have left unattended and for which women have not assumed sufficient responsibility. It is an area into which the cultural attributes of women can be used to their fullest. The field is wide open. It compares in this way with the wide-open land in colonial days, when there was so much work to be done that there was no sex limitation on who did it.

At the same time that scientific development has made endless housekeeping chores obsolete, it has

[1] *Self and Society: Social Change and Individual Development* (New York: Atherton Press, 1966), pp. 270-71.

94

magnified the need in the world for feminine care —as a symbol of love, reconciliation, and sensitivity. The time has come for women to enlarge their circle of concern to include the community. (Our responsibility, of course, is not limited to the local community, but if we aim for the world, we are liable to limit our action to talking about the problems over coffee!) Significant involvement on a community level calls for the same qualities we have developed in caring for our families. Instead of trying to change these characteristics, we can broaden our base of concern. Our care can encompass those beyond our own nuclear family. Our attempts to reconcile can extend to the alienated of society. Our sensitivity can reach outside our doorway to the environmentally handicapped. We need not live in the past and play house all day, nor denounce our femininity to imitate masculinity. We can accept our sex without questioning our significance. In moving beyond feminism, we can use all the qualities at our disposal to create a new community.

Our task would be easier if someone could provide a mass plan so that in simply following steps one, two, and three, we could develop model communities. The problem is much more complex. The local specifics get in the way. The specific strengths and weaknesses of a local community cannot be generalized. Ideas can be taken from other localities and from writings, but they must be adapted to each local situation to be effective.

Just as communities have a range of different needs and resources, we have a variety of interests and abilities. We need to have a holistic understanding of our particular community and its needs, as well as a grasp of our own competencies, before we can make a knowledgeable decision about the object and direction of our energies. We may want to learn about the community on an individual basis, or we may prefer a neighborhood or church study-action group. During the study, we can make a list of priorities, and then each of us can find the niche that fits our interests and abilities.

There is a story about Andrew Carnegie in which he was asked to meet the deficit of a national symphony orchestra. He suggested that they raise half the money from other donors, and then he would contribute the remainder. A short time later the chairman told him they had the money. Mr. Carnegie was pleased, and when he asked the chairman where they had gotten it, he was informed that *Mrs.* Carnegie had given it.

Most of us cannot help sufficiently through financial donations. We will need to contribute ourselves as well. But how do we get started? By taking seriously his church's study-action group on "Social Issues and the Individual," a layman stated in a letter to the pastor[2] that applying some techniques used elsewhere might be helpful to churchmen seeking to meet today's needs. He suggested the following guidelines:

1. Make a commitment.
2. Set goals which can be accomplished.

[2] The letter, dated March 30, 1970, was written by Mr. C. F. Moore, Jr., chairman of the Administrative Board of St. Stephen's United Methodist Church.

96

3. Take the responsibility upon yourself.
4. Be specific.
5. Decide on a plan of action.
6. Make periodic reviews.
7. Don't give up.

These guidelines don't promise solutions, but they show us how to become involved in the struggle for a better world. Beyond this, the writing of the letter is in itself an example of taking study and commitment seriously.

The kinds of jobs that need to be done in the community, both paid and volunteer, should be seen holistically. Each one is important to the accomplishment of the task. Perhaps one of our contributions can be toward more effective community management. The men have left us with a hierarchical model of management with executives at the top, administrators on the next level, managers on the next, etc. Perhaps we can build a new model in which, instead of a vertical ladder of positions, we have a horizontal chain, and each niche is seen as necessary to the whole. The dreamers, innovators, and task forces—the paid and unpaid—could all work together in the struggle to develop new community structures and humanize existing ones.

Women can fill needs in a variety of areas. The role of wife and mother is basic but not all-encompassing. We are needed in organized civic and professional groups, in business and industry (in both management and labor), and in government and politics. We are needed in sociology, city planning, community mental health, school planning. The issues of war, increasing juvenile delinquency, poor educational opportunities, unemployment, pollution, race relations, and social renewal call for our attention. Both sensitivity and reconciliation are needed if we are to build alternatives to the urban jungle and the suburban rat race.

If we are to enlarge our circle of concern, our involvement in elections cannot be overlooked. There are over three million more women than men in this country, but men outnumber women in terms of voting.[3] One of our imperatives is the responsible use of the power of the ballot. But even this is not always enough. Our concern and effectiveness in the domestic realm as wives and mothers can be broadened to affect the community realm as city officials. If a woman is qualified for public office, it is her responsibility to seek election or appointment to it—and ours to support her. Following are some guidelines. Before seeking office, a woman should:

1. Know her community; work hard on community affairs.
2. Acquire a knowledge of government by observing and by lobbying for causes in which she is interested.
3. Do some work for her party; raise some money; make a contribution herself.
4. Learn the rules. How are nominations made? When and by whom?
5. Learn all she can about the office she seeks. Let

[3] Brenton, *The American Male*, p. 77.

party officials know she is interested in running. Not wait to be asked.

During the campaign, she should:

1. Be willing to work hard. Knock on every door.
2. Get a strong committee going for her. Women make good campaign workers, but she should have men on her committee too.
3. Listen to people. Find out what they are interested in, what their problems are.
4. Be willing to work harder than those she is running against or working with after the election.

After election (hopefully), she should:

1. Listen and look but speak only when she knows what she is talking about.
2. Be a lady. Be friendly but businesslike with male colleagues. Not be competitive; work with them.
3. Be willing to sacrifice other activities if she wants to do a thorough and excellent job.
4. Not try to make over the world too fast.
5. Do what she thinks is right and not be sensitive or "have her feelings hurt."
6. Develop her own particular interests and work hard at learning about them.[4]

It is difficult for us to overcome the time-honored idea that we are just enablers for men. But in today's world we are needed not only behind, but also beside men (and sometimes in front of them) in the struggle to create a better world. Our place is anywhere that our abilities meet humanity's needs.

The idea of women in positions of government is

[4] "Women and Politics," *Feminine Focus*, III (March, 1968), 4, 7.

hardly new. Plato recognized the necessity of selecting "duly qualified women also, to share in the life and official labours of the duly qualified men." But putting this into practice in our country is relatively new. The first woman member of the House of Representatives was Jeanette Rankin, who was sent from Montana in 1917. She served two non-consecutive periods, during which she voted against America's entrance into both world wars. At 82, she returned to Washington to lead the Jeanette Rankin Brigade in protest of United States involvement in Vietnam.[5] The first woman to serve in the Senate was Mrs. Rebecca Latimer Felton of Georgia, who was appointed in 1922 to serve one day. Ten years later, Hattie W. Caraway was appointed to fill her husband's term and was subsequently elected.[6] Frances Perkins, FDR's Secretary of Labor, was the first woman to hold a Cabinet position.[7] One of the benefits of community experience can be the branching out into state, national, and international government.

Women can make a unique contribution in the area of city government and planning. One of the common problems of communities across the country is quality child care. Men have less opportunity than we do to develop sensitivity in this area. We need to be more responsible on a broader basis than we have been in the past. Those of us who feel that

[5] Peggy Lamson, *Few Are Chosen: American Women in Political Life Today* (Boston: Houghton Mifflin Company, 1968), p. xxvii.

[6] *Ibid.*

[7] *American Women*, p. 65.

100

a mother's presence is important to the preschooler have tended to judge the salaried mother with small children. We have limited our circle of concern to our own family and the well-being of our children. To enlarge our concern is to include the well-being of all the children in the community. It becomes our responsibility to see that child care facilities move beyond the dimension of convenience into the dimension of excellence. While over half the children of working mothers are cared for at home, nearly a fourth are cared for away from home, and eight percent receive *no care at all!* [8]

We can also be sensitive to the needs of older children. Our concern for children from lower socioeconomic backgrounds to have opportunities equal to those of our own children can help remedy, and perhaps prevent, some of the situations which cause juvenile delinquency. These children need to have available as many of the experiences from which our children benefit as possible. An example is our children's summertime joy in community parks and swimming pools. We can work toward placing new pools and parks where they will be easily accessible to the children from poverty areas. In the meantime, we can attempt to work out transportation for them and perhaps free swimming lessons.

Drug abuse is another problem of youth that has spread. Some of us could take it upon ourselves to see that *every* teenager within the community is

[8] "Children of Working Mothers," U.S. Department of Health, Education, and Welfare, Children's Bureau, 1960, Bulletin 382: 57% cared for at home; 22% cared for away from home; 13% other; 8% no care.

101

exposed to information about its dangers. This could be done through the church, the P.T.A., community recreation centers, or youth organizations.

The improvement of race relations must be a priority of responsible community leaders. Women have a history of being actively concerned about racial equality. The complexity of this problem has increased over the past few years. We could once strive for integration, but now there is a cry for separate equality. One way to gain insight is through group discussions *with*, not *about*, Blacks (or whites). At a meeting in which a mixed panel discussed "The Black Manifesto," a black sociologist stated: "If there is change, it will be due to white women deciding to change a nation. If we leave it to white men, it won't be done."

Education is a vital realm. Volunteer or semi–volunteer aides are needed in the public schools. These should be persons with the qualities of warmth and sensitivity, a spontaneous ability to relate to people, a noncompetitive attitude toward teachers, and a genuine interest in children. In Rochester, New York, aides are used in early elementary school. After a short training period, they give individual attention to children with mild or moderate problems that could become chronic or profound if ignored.[9] This is an excellent means of involvement for two groups: retired people (aides have ranged from sixty-five to eighty years old), and mothers who want to be home when their school-age children are.

[9] Emory Cowen, "Mothers in the Classroom," *Psychology Today*, III (December, 1969), 36-39.

Women are also needed in administration and curriculum development, as teachers, counselors, educational consultants, and schoolboard members. We are needed in positions of educational responsibility that range from local to national influence. We can work for the passing of educational bills that will shrink class size, provide adequate teaching equipment, and finance efforts to meet local specific needs. We can work toward the goal that when the national budget is made, our children get the largest slice of the pie. According to Gardner:

The educational system provides the young person with a sense of what society expects of him in the way of performance. If it is lax in its demands, then he will believe that such are the expectations of his society. If much is expected of him, the chances are that he will expect much of himself.[10]

Women can work toward the enhancement of self-expectations and the possibility of their fulfillment for all the children of the community.

An area of concern that spreads throughout the world community is overpopulation. (But with four children, I feel hypocritical in writing about this problem!) The other day our last-born ran to the door to greet Bill when he came home from work, calling "Daddy! Daddy! Hug!" Bill picked him up and looked at me and said, "I'm so glad he was born before we realized we were immoral!"

What a joy our children are, and how grateful we are for them! But the fact remains that we have filled more than our share of the people-spaces on

[10] *Self-Renewal*, p. 20.

our planet. When we discuss overpopulation within the family, we express our delight in having four lovely children, but at the same time we stress the imperative that they have no more than two. We have talked about the responsible alternative of adopting children if they decide they want larger families.

The feminine responsibility in regard to overpopulation is, first of all, to stop having babies! Our laws hark back to the pioneer days when it was important to the country that we "go forth and multiply." Now it is important that we simply "go forth." We have the scientific knowledge to plan if and when we will have children. As overpopulation is a crisis, it has become vital that we employ every means of birth control at our disposal. We need to think beyond the traditional contraceptives. Paul Ehrlich, in *The Population Bomb*, suggests that biologists must "point out the biological absurdity of equating a zygote or fetus with a human being." [11] Abortion, tubal ligation, and vasectomy need to be seriously considered as options to the immorality of producing unplanned and unwanted additions to the masses of humanity.

Another world concern is peace. A woman dedicated to full equality for women wrote an article entitled: "Let's Draft Women, Too." [12] But if we are to move beyond feminism, I cannot see spending our energies to get our daughters drafted, but instead, to give our sons the opportunity to live in

[11] (New York: Ballantine Books, 1968), p. 147.
[12] Caroline Bird, "Let's Draft Women, Too," *The Saturday Evening Post* (June 18, 1966), 10 ff.

peace. In addressing the 1969 AAUW Convention, Martha Peterson, president of Barnard College, said: "We cannot continue to bear sons whose lives will be snuffed out on the eve of their flowering. War is archaic and obsolete." [13] We must strive as hard to move toward a meaningful peace as our men do to "save face."

My youngest child, Bryant, had said nothing but "doggie" until he was almost two years old. Early one morning he became disgusted with me for not getting him out of his crib when he was ready, and he said clearly and distinctly: "Hurry up, Mommy." This is the word to the woman of faith. Matthew Arnold once said, "If ever we see a time when the women of the world come together purely and solely for the benefit of mankind, no force in the universe can stop them." The time is now!

[13] "The Responsibility of the Educated Woman," *AAUW Journal* (October, 1969), 6.

9

THE CHRISTIAN FEMINIST

When we married, many of us followed the tradition of carrying something old, something new, something borrowed, something blue. Life is a combination of the old and the new, of the traditional and the contemporary. We live in a time in which women are carrying, along with an old regard for femininity, a new emphasis on equal responsibility. We want to stand *with* the men who are willing to stand up and be counted in our pre–twenty-first century world.

A major event in a woman's life is choosing her vocation. This is a fairly new event in the history of woman—for she has traditionally chosen a husband rather than a vocation. Now she can choose either or both. The event of choosing a vocation represents the importance of autonomy. It is an expression of self-determination. It is an effort toward independence and self-assertiveness in an expanding, personal world. It is with this sense of autonomy that she stands as a free and responsible human being. Choosing a vocation is a symbol of her responsibility to help create conditions conducive to the recognition of individual significance around the globe. She acts out this responsibility within her own community. She recognizes the uniqueness and worth of others and supports their struggle for individuality. She understands the need for respect and dignity for all the members of her community; she understands their need for the power to be self-directing and their dream of self-actualization. As a Christian feminist, if this is where her interests and abilities lie, she commits herself to this area of social renewal.

Another major event in a woman's life is marriage. The pre–twenty-first century woman is free to choose *not* to marry—just as man has always been free to make this choice. The event of marriage represents the importance of relatedness. It is an expression of self-surrender. It is an effort toward interdependence and self-giving. It is with this sense of relatedness that she involves herself in corporate action with other free and responsible human beings. Marriage is a symbol of her responsibility to help create conditions conducive to the development of meaningful relationships around the globe. She acts out this responsibility within her own community. She recognizes the significant place of each person in the whole. She understands the need for finding ways of relating to the separated, alienated, deviant, delinquent—the lonely members—of her community. She looks for the empty singer and listens for the silent song. She sees and hears, and as a Christian feminist, if this is where her interests and abilities lie, she commits herself to singing with him.

107

A common and yet unique experience for woman is the birth of a baby. She feels this life within her—and then she holds this tiny human being. Two eyes—they see! Two ears—they hear! A lovely nose and hungry mouth, two thrashing arms and little legs, ten clutching fingers and tiny toes—all there! It is miraculous! He comes into the world crying, but she teaches him to laugh. The event of birth represents the preciousness of life itself. This warm helpless lovely new life is a symbol of her responsibility for all the babies born around the globe. She acts out her responsibility within her own community. What she wants for her own child, she desires on a community level to benefit all the children therein. Food and shelter and proper medical care, but also quality education, cultural experiences, safe places to play, museums, zoos, parks, swimming pools—these are her realm, but they are considered from a broad perspective. As a Christian feminist, if this is where her interests and abilities lie, she commits herself to an open-ended future for *all* children.

Finally, an event that steps into life to devastate and destroy, to call our security into question and our anxiety to the fore, is death—the death of a parent or friend or husband or child. The event of death is the ultimate *no*. It represents the limitation, the restriction, the finality that border one's life. But death is a symbol of the ultimate *yes*. To say yes is to choose *life* within the boundaries of one's life-space; it is to affirm life on whatever terms it is offered. It is to accept its reality, its relatedness, its responsibilities. To choose life is to be alert and sensitive to the here and the now. The Christian feminist feels and sees and hears and smells and tastes life to the fullest—and she risks herself for the sake of another.

To move beyond feminism is to celebrate these old events—vocation, marriage, childbirth, death—with a new dimension. It is to dream of autonomous persons willing to give themselves in authentic relatedness, who know the value of each life, and whose life-space proclaims the ultimate yes.

To move beyond feminism is to work toward the creation of the kind of world where this is possible. In *The Fratricides*, Father Yánaros laughs with his friend and says: "The world, Andreas, is being formed every day. It's being remodeled every day; don't despair; who knows, perhaps one morning God will call upon you to create the world you have in mind." [1] But the laughter between them is inappropriate. God *is* calling each of us to create the world we have in mind. Not only technologically, but also humanly. We are free and responsible. We can imagine and create. We can dream a dream and commit ourselves to it. We can dream of a more meaningful life for ourselves; we can dream of a better life for another; we can dream of a world advancing in understanding, in values, in excellence. We can dream of reaching full humanness in a fully human world.

As we strive toward these dreams, the most difficult aspect of all is that the struggle will not cease. For these dreams are unattainable. There are those who say that people cannot struggle for unattainable

[1] Kazantzakis, *The Fratricides*, p. 215.

goals without finally falling into utter despair and giving up. But there has always been that remnant of committed persons who proved them wrong. The woman of faith must always remember that success is measured, not only by the achievement of small goals, but also by the intensity of the struggle toward impossible ones.

The Christian feminist is not dependent upon her husband and children for her identity. She hears the summons to today's woman and dares to say "I."

He who says "I" has said everything. Just as every man contains all men, this word contains all words. It is the only word God uttered at Mount Sinai. Yet one must know how to pronounce it as He does. He says "I" and it means: I who am with you, within you. We say "I" and it means: I who am opposed to you, all of you. His "I" embraces men, ours divides them. On His lips "I" means love, on ours too, but it is no longer the same love.[2]

The Christian feminist strives to learn how to pronounce "I" as God does. She sees love as involved care. And it is this love in action which moves her beyond feminism. For the Christian feminist dares to place her "I" in the "we" of her community, her nation, her world. She celebrates the past as it was, freely confronts the present as it is, and assumes responsibility for the future. In the spirit of Christ, she heeds the challenge of these crucial times and hurls herself into history, struggling to bend it in the direction of hope.

[2] Elie Wiesel, *A Beggar in Jerusalem* (New York: Random House, 1970), p. 7.

110

BIBLIOGRAPHY

American Women. Report of the President's Commission on the Status of Women, 1963.

Berne, Eric. *Games People Play: The Psychology of Human Relationships*. New York: Grove Press, 1964.

Bird, Caroline. *Born Female: The High Cost of Keeping Women Down*. New York: David McKay Company, 1968.

Brenton, Myron. *The American Male*. New York: Coward-McCann, 1966.

Catt, Carrie Chapman, and Shuler, Nettie Rogers. *Woman Suffrage and Politics*. New York: Charles Scribner's Sons, 1926.

de Beauvoir, Simone. *The Second Sex*. New York: Alfred A. Knopf, 1957.

Ehrlich, Paul R. *The Population Bomb*. New York: Ballantine Books, 1968.

Frankl, Viktor. *From Death-Camp to Existentialism*, trans. Ilse Lasch. Boston: Beacon Press, 1959.

———. *Man's Search for Meaning*, trans. Ilse Lasch. Boston: Beacon Press, 1962.

———. *The Doctor and the Soul*. New York: Alfred A. Knopf, 1955.

Friedan, Betty. *The Feminine Mystique*. New York: Dell Publishing Company, 1963.

Fromm, Erich. *Escape from Freedom*. New York: Rinehart & Company, 1941.

———. *The Art of Loving*. New York: Bantam Books, 1963.

Gardner, John W. *Self-Renewal: The Individual and the Innovative Society*. New York: Harper Colophon ed., Harper & Row, 1965.

Ginzberg, Eli. *Life Styles of Educated Women*. New York: Columbia University Press, 1966.

Gunner, Myrdal. *An American Dilemma*. New York: Harper & Row, 1963.

Lamson, Peggy. *Few Are Chosen: American Women in Political Life Today*. Boston: Houghton Mifflin Company, 1968.

May, Rollo. *Love and Will*. New York: W. W. Norton & Company, 1969.

Mead, Margaret. *Male and Female*. New York: William Morrow & Company, 1949.

Money, John. "Developmental Differentiation of Femininity and Masculinity Compared." Farber, Seymour, and Wilson, Roger H. L., eds. *The Potential of Women*. New York: McGraw-Hill Book Company, 1963.

Newcomer, Mabel. *A Century of Higher Education for American Women*. New York: Harper & Brothers, 1959.

Nye, F. Ivan, and Hoffman, Lois W. *The Employed Mother in America*. Chicago: Rand McNally & Company, 1963.

Sanford, Nevitt. *Self and Society: Social Change and Individual Development*. New York: Atherton Press, 1966.

Sartre, Jean-Paul. *Existentialism*, trans. Bernard Frectman. New York: Philosophical Library, 1947.

Scott, Ann Firor. "Women and Men," Underwood, Kenneth, ed., *The Church, The University, and Social Policy*. The Danforth Study of Campus Ministries, Vol. II. Middletown, Conn.: Wesleyan University Press, 1969.

Tillich, Paul. *The Courage to Be*. New Haven: Yale University Press, 1952.

————. *The Shaking of the Foundations*. New York: Charles Scribner's Sons, 1948.

Victory: How Women Won It. A Centennial Symposium by The National American Woman Suffrage Association. New York: The H. W. Wilson Company, 1940.

Woody, Thomas. *A History of Women's Education in the United States*. Vol. II. New York: The Science Press, 1929.